critical essays in modern literature

The Hero in Hemingway's Short Stories

BY JOSEPH DEFALCO

Pitt Paperback—13

CRITICAL ESSAYS IN MODERN LITERATURE

Critical Essays in Modern Literature

THE HERO IN HEMINGWAY'S SHORT STORIES

THE
HERO
IN
HEMINGWAY'S
SHORT
STORIES

by Joseph DeFalco

University of Pittsburgh Press

To My Wife

Acknowledgment

I WISH TO RECORD MY GRATITUDE to those who have given me encouragement and counsel in the writing of this book: in particular, to Harry R. Warfel, under whose guidance this work was originally written, and whose friendship and understanding contributed more than he can know; to Charles W. Morris, who assisted me in my study of Jung's works; to David Stryker, Stephen F. Fogel, and John A. Penrod, who invested their time and patience and good will; to William Bysshe Stein, whose friendly advice provided needed stimulation at many points; and to Edwin M. Moseley, who introduced Hemingway's work to me a long time ago.

For permission to quote from each of the following works I am grateful to the publisher, Charles Scribner's Sons: *The Short Stories of Ernest Hemingway, Death in the Afternoon,* and *Green Hills of Africa.* Quotations from "Two Tales of Darkness," which appeared in *The Atlantic Monthly,* are used with the kind permission of Mrs. Hemingway. In addition, the following have granted permission to quote from the works cited: Holt, Rinehart and Winston, Philip Young's *Ernest Hemingway;* Harcourt, Brace & World, T. S. Eliot's "The Wasteland" in *The Complete Poems and Plays*, and Carl G. Jung's *Modern Man in Search of a Soul;* Peter Smith, Jessie L. Weston's *From Ritual to Romance;* and *The American Imago*, James Clark Maloney's "The Origin of the Rejected and Crippled Hero Myths." Other copyrighted material appears herein under the "Resolution on Permissions" of the Association of American University Presses.

Table of Contents

Introduction

THE ADVENT OF MODERN PSYCHOANALYTICAL procedures has exerted an unquestionable influence upon literary criticism. This study utilizes many of the insights provided by these procedures in the examination of the short stories of Ernest Hemingway. Although the author of this work is informed principally by the works of Carl G. Jung, there is no attempt to follow rigidly any specific part of his theory. Since this study focuses chiefly upon individual stories, the story itself is always the determiner in the formulation of patterns of interpretation. Conventional critical materials have not been avoided, for many times they bolster the psychological premises.

The structure of Hemingway's stories (and the dominant motifs they employ) correlates with his openly avowed intent to translate factual data into fiction in order to recreate the essence of true-life experience. This method combined with his belief in certain elemental patterns of human action and thought to become the means by which his art achieved its expression. These patterns relate to this study insofar as they illuminate the motivations and responses of the central characters of the stories. For what

1

Hemingway does, essentially, is to catalogue the disillusionments of contemporary man in his struggle to come to terms with a world he cannot truly understand.

The implications of this continuing challenge provide the central conflict in many of the stories. As the characters demonstrate, the possibility of understanding and overcoming the contingencies in life are small. Feats of heroic magnitude are demanded of the individual, but not everyone is capable of the effort. Although most of Hemingway's heroes fail, the successful few emerge as heroes of a different stature. For them triumph amounts to crucifixion, and on these occasions the vehicle of the crucified-god motif mediates their fate. As Hemingway orders life in these stories, those who master and control the contingencies of life die; those who cannot overcome these dislocations resort to compromise, and they become the "adjusted" ones. Those who can neither compromise nor conquer are the alienated and isolated ones, and in their moral cowardice they waste away in utter deracination.

Hemingway's view of this plight of mankind is best observed when the stories are placed in a sequential arrangement according to the age of the main characters or according to the type of experience they undergo. Such an arrangement necessarily violates the chronology according to publication dates, but a demonstrable pattern of thematic and structural coherence results. One of the outstanding themes which emerges is that of individuation, or the quest for self-illumination. In the early stories whenever a character like Nick Adams leaves the comfort and security of home or when he discovers that comfort and security at home are illusory, he is thrust into his first encounter with the forces of contingency. These early conflicts are initiatory in nature, and subsequently they generate the tensions of the long and arduous journey towards understanding. The complete journey of Nick Adams is not contained in a full cycle of stories; rather his ultimate destiny is involved with that of the other characters. All are to some extent victims of the same plight, and Nick's fate can be judged according to the reactions of characters with a similar background.

The emphasis throughout this study is always upon examining the relationship between structure and theme. Psychological symbolism provides the means whereby the nature of this relationship may be explored. Whether the symbolic function of details reveals itself through the use of characters, episodes, patterns of imagery, or in isolated symbols, these always integrate with the plot structure and contribute to thematic design. Hemingway recognizes that each is not a separate entity, and he organizes his materials so that each is part of an organic whole. This unity of structure projects the implications of a character's struggle with life into the realm of the psychological conflicts of all men.

Chapter I

The Quest for a Literary Ideal

IN ANY WORK OF FICTION the artist must solve the problems of selecting a vehicle to carry his theme. The choice may be fortunate or unfortunate, depending upon his degree of skill. The ordinary mechanical devices he uses may further the literal development of plot, but unless these serve the organic purpose of developing theme, the craftsmanship is deficient. No true artist overlooks the necessity of integrating all of the elements of formal execution, for the functional relevancy of the materials he employs becomes the index of the over-all unity in his work.

Ultimately, of course, if the artistic order of a work has been adequately sustained, it is impossible to separate the internal dynamics of form from the thematic design itself. Both are mutually supporting and interpenetrative, taking their vitality one from another in such a manner that any attempt at isolation of one results in the diminished significance of its complement. Moreover, due regard to the coequality of the two as fictive processes leads to a more coherent understanding of a work as an artistic totality. The sublimation of mode and idea, of form and theme, is the final test of the true artistic worth in any imaginative work.

Fiction as an imaginative dramatization of ideas must conform to the implications of its nature. In America the products of fictional endeavor are numerous, but only in a few is the union and harmony of the structural and the conceptual apparent. Melville's *Moby-Dick,* Hawthorne's *The Scarlet Letter,* and Twain's *Adventures of Huckleberry Finn* are among the works of the past that have exhibited such harmony, and they are among America's greatest literary achievements.

Close examination of the works of these three authors demonstrates that each was a master in selecting the vehicle best suited to project his theme. There would be no point in viewing *Adventures of Huckleberry Finn* simply as a story of a boy on a raft floating down a river. Such a surface examination overlooks the important facts that Twain carefully structured his story on the journey artifice and that Huck's development as a moral and ethical agent is an inherent part of a universal pattern. It would be equally inconsequential to designate *Moby-Dick* as a story solely about whaling, or *The Scarlet Letter* as a description of life in early Puritan Boston. These novels are considerably more, and what makes them more is the skill employed by the artist in evolving the vehicles for conveying theme.

Each of these novels has a framework that is much more than surface outline or simple plot structure. In *Adventures of Huckleberry Finn* such an outline might take cognizance of the episodic structure, but it would surely miss the correlative, mythological and psychological journey that translates the local into the universal. These more significant meanings, not immediately apparent on the surface, give the work thematic depth and project what otherwise might be a superficial whim or ideal of an author into the sphere of the primordial conflicts of all men. The ability of an author to so mold his framework that the reader is constantly subjected to forces beyond the mere transitory nuances of surface conflict inevitably determines the degree of importance in a work of art. When he can accomplish such an amalgamation of materials, the result makes for permanence in the art form.

All art strives for permanence, and the degree of its success centers in no small measure on the artist's ability to penetrate beyond surface reality into the realm of universal human experience. As many efforts to realize the true in art have been made as there have been great artists, and only those authors who have approached truth in their art have escaped obscurity. Theories of art and aesthetics are plentiful. Since the time of Plato and Aristotle theorists have striven to characterize the essential elements in a work of art that explain its ability to transcend the world of the personal and finite into that of the transpersonal and infinite. Whether or not any systematic theory has adequately crystallized the nature of aesthetic theory is of no real consequence, however, when dealing with an individual artist and the body of his work. Each creative artist has his own private sensitivity and mode of dealing with his material, and each seeks to answer questions about certain basic problems of all mankind according to his own peculiar outlook. The focus upon an individual artist's method of dealing with these problems and on the problems themselves leads the reader to an understanding of a work beyond mere elementary impression. The degree of insight a reader may have into the structural and thematic relationships of a particular work determines his critical apprehension of a work as a unique achievement and, perhaps, as an artistic success.

Although many artists have written about their craft, only a few have approached a systematic crystallization of their ideas and attitudes about it. Creative artists generally interest themselves primarily in that order of creativity which produces ideas in dramatic form rather than articulation of ideas in pure intellectual expression. With few exceptions, however, major writers have addressed themselves to the subject of their craft, at least fragmentarily, both in and out of their fictional compositions. Many times their commentaries are illuminating in relation to their own art and to art in general, and always these expressions merit serious consideration.

In the works of Ernest Hemingway both the overt and implied statements about art and aesthetic theory are fragmentary. As a guide to the understanding of certain basic aesthetic techniques and aims in his fiction, these revelations are not of less significance because they are not systematized. On the contrary, a full understanding of Hemingway's artistry may come about by an examination of his fictional achievement in the light of his direct statements about his art and its meaning. A focus on an artist's intent is not the sole approach to an understanding of his work, for some authors have created much that is beyond their own ken. Yet if the artist who has created the works at hand states a conscious intent, his theorizing might reveal the major emphasis of his thought. From this perspective, viewing some of Hemingway's attitudes toward his work directs the reader to a clearer understanding of his conscious artistry.

Because of a certain bias in the Hemingway personality, it is difficult to screen the serious from the ironic in the tabloid accounts of his statements about the craft of writing. But a number of recurring expressions and attitudes in his own work merit serious consideration. His most important dicta occur in his two early nonfictional works, *Death in the Afternoon* and *Green Hills of Africa*. Since these books take as their subjects bullfighting and big game hunting, respectively, it is not to be expected that any direct and systematic analysis of the artistic method is attempted in them. What becomes apparent is that the attitudes of Hemingway the bullfight *aficionado* and Hemingway the hunting enthusiast are never far removed from those of Hemingway the author and aesthetician.

In both of the nonfictional works, using the analogy of a good bullfighter or hunter as an ideal, Hemingway describes the attitudes of a good writer. In this way he suggests that the prime target of every writer ought to be the achievement of that degree of permanence of which his art is capable. For Hemingway this victory can come only to the writers of "classics." In the discussion of such writers he reveals his own strivings and suggests the direction his own art was to point: "A new classic does not bear any resemblance to the classics that have preceded it. It can steal from anything that it is better than, anything that is not a classic, all classics do that. Some writers are born only to help another writer to write one sentence. But it cannot derive from or resemble a previous classic." [1] Aside from the obvious charge brought by Hemingway's detractors that such passages are meant to remove some of the stigma from the attacks Gertrude Stein had made for his borrowings from contemporaries, there is discernible here an indication that a writer must have the same interest and intensity of purpose that marks the great bullfighter and hunter. This opinion is of significance, for such commentaries directly suggest Hemingway's conscious pursuit of a literary ideal.

A further reflection of this pursuit is exhibited in a passage in which Hemingway discusses his own reaction to the works of Turgenev. Describing the feeling of having been physically present in the real and fictional places in the novels, Hemingway suggests that if one can achieve such effects in art he will have realized perhaps the greatest of all human desires — a kind of personal immortality: "A country, finally, erodes and the dust blows away, the people all die and none of them were of any importance permanently, except those who practised the arts. . . . A thousand years makes economics silly and a work of art endures forever." [2]

In *Death in the Afternoon,* the earlier of the two nonfiction works, Hemingway specifically reveals the origin of his purpose and the apprenticeship that led to the final accomplishments of the later works.

In direct accounts his early tendency toward seeking "truth" in fiction is revealed: "I was trying to write then and I found the greatest difficulty, aside from knowing truly what you really felt, rather than what you were supposed to feel, and had been taught to feel, was to put down what really happened in action; what the actual things were which produced the emotion that you experienced." [3] Although such articulations were responsible for the now shopworn commentaries about "the way it was," Hemingway is sincere and gives serious importance to the need for translating the totality of real life events into art. Always he emphasizes the need to capture the essence of the varied complexities that go to make up real-life experiences. These statements of purpose when fully examined reveal the *raison d'etre* of Hemingway's art and his calculated goal of experimentation with fictional techniques whereby the artistic reflection would legitimately shape the real-life experiences into the mold of art. Art for Hemingway is not a mere copy of life. Almost in the sense of what Sidney demanded, it is that which seeks to incorporate those elements from experience that are "truer . . . than anything factual can be." [4]

The qualities that can be extracted from real life and united with fictional forms are, for Hemingway, the basis of the aesthetic posture of art as opposed to mere writing. Once the writer has found the secret of creating in this fashion he will have approached the goal that Hemingway indicates he had set for himself: finding "the real thing, the sequence of motion and fact which made the emotion and which would be as valid in a year or in ten years or, with

luck and if you stated it purely enough, always." [5]
That is, permanence in art can be achieved through
such an aesthetic if the artist is "serious enough and
has luck" and can get beyond a flat, three dimen-
sional imitation of actuality into the sphere of the
"fourth and fifth dimension" of a pure art form. [6]

Such piecemeal commentaries scattered throughout his nonfictional works demonstrate Hemingway's
fundamental concern with an aesthetic theory. They
further illustrate his desire to free himself from conventional techniques and forge a new and vibrant
artistry in his chosen craft. How well he succeeded
may be seen only in an examination of some of the
actual techniques he selected to attain his goal.

Chapter II

The Hero as Symbol

IN THE ATTEMPT TO GET AT THE "TRUTH" of real-life experience and to attain the ideal of writing a "classic" that he initially posed for himself, Hemingway began in his early volumes of short stories to describe the adventures of a boy on the threshold of manhood. As Philip Young and Carlos Baker have pointed out in their studies, half of the stories of *In Our Time* (1925), the first short story collection, are devoted to the development of Nick Adams.[1] They are arranged chronologically, moving from Nick's boyhood to his young manhood, and all of these stories are thematically related. Several more stories about the same character appear in the next two collections, *Men Without Women* (1927) and *Winner Take Nothing* (1933). Of importance to the whole of Hemingway's fiction is this early focus on a young hero, for if Philip Young is correct, this hero is to become the prototype "Hemingway Hero" who later will have essentially the same background that Nick has had through his childhood, adolescence, and young manhood. More important than a mere similarity of background in the successive protagonists is the resemblance they bear to

13

each other psychologically. All experience the same needs in meeting the struggle and frustration of twentieth-century man, and even of all men of all times. Some become involved in war, suffer wounds, and are forced to reconcile the psychological disturbances created by these hurts. Others are forced to come to terms with the reality of the traumata created by the pressures of a hostile environment.

In *Death in the Afternoon* Hemingway refers to himself as a naturalist of the kind that Thoreau was in his observations of nature. The comparison is a good one, for both differ from the scientific observer who focuses upon the botanical or zoological significance of the external and material substances of the world. In his fiction Hemingway examines the effect upon the inner being of the traumata that modern man has experienced in the world. This attempt to get beyond surface manifestations and deal with more basic, primal contexts led Hemingway to apply certain distinct, psychologically symbolic techniques in his fiction. When these work for him, the entire tone and texture of his prose comes to a close approximation of the "classic" he always tried to write.

At the outset, Hemingway gives Nick Adams and the other protagonists a responsive sensibility. This technique is not a simple device of characterization intended solely to illuminate the character's inner feelings. More expansive, it parallels the questioning attitude that heroes have exhibited in literature since Homer shaped the epic form. Homer forged into two epic works the whole of Greek thought and culture. Just as his heroes in their victories and defeats represented the needs and drives and experiences of that culture, so Hemingway has for the twentieth century attempted to expand the significance of the experiences of his protagonists into a range far exceeding local and subjective considerations of ordinary fictional conflict. In short, he has tried to write "classics" by capturing the tone and tensions of his own culture.

As his organizing principle, Hemingway chose to depict a series of heroes who become progressively older and experience both literally and psychologically what all men of the twentieth century have experienced over a period of almost fifty years. When these heroes seem unusually introspective and the themes seem too narrow and local, Hemingway may have failed as a craftsman, but he has not lost sight of his ideals. Even in those works where he has been criticized most for organizational failures, one step further in his overall plan has been developed. This plan to view man's relationship to his culture, to the other men in that culture, and ultimately to the cosmos, he carefully develops throughout his short stories. An investigation of this pattern in them reveals the substance of an underlying organization which is the core of his artistry.

In the short stories focusing on Nick Adams and in the other short stories of the three collections, inner attitudes are externalized by means of symbolic reflection. These symbolizations manifest themselves in a variety of conventional ways, but they also appear in unique and quite unexpected combinations. Sometimes characters represent particular attitudes, or episodes point up conflicts, or a sequence of images is repeated a sufficient number of times to create symbolic formations; many times there is a major, controlling symbol from which all of the details take their meaning. One of the most important symbolizations takes the form of a ritualization of a familiar activity, thereby objectifying the intense struggle of the characters in their attempt to find a solution to their inner turmoil. In this way Hemingway maintains a studied control over his material, and this careful control forms a contrast to the content. Ordered artistry is always juxtaposed to the chaos in which most of the central characters find themselves.

In the development of Nick Adams as the leading protagonist in the early short stories, Hemingway utilizes one of his most significant symbolic devices to project his themes. This is the journey artifice. In one sense, all of Hemingway's works employ some aspect of this motif. The Hemingway hero may never bear much literal resemblance to Odysseus as a classical hero, but his encounters with the bitter but always illuminating experiences of life, and his journey through life itself, are analogous to the classical journey motif. Hemingway's use of this framework enables the thematic conflicts in the stories to ramify beyond the immediate literal level of individual and sociological considerations into the sphere of the primordial, psychological conflicts of every man.

The intense inner conflicts of the Hemingway protagonist are revealed many times directly by means of correlative mythological or psychological symbols which parallel the surface action. It is here that any study of the process of symbolization and its manifold associative connotations should begin. Further, by examining Hemingway's symbolism the development of the hero and the accompanying, implied theme of individuation may be seen from a perspective which illuminates the methodology of all the works.

In fact, most of the psychological and mythological symbolism that may be analyzed in Hemingway's fiction can be associated with the journey artifice. As a device it is as old as mankind. Evidence for this motif has been found by anthropologists in the most primitive cultures, and its use in the early epic formula is based on verbal and experiential data that precedes man's ability to even articulate his problems. In *The Hero with a Thousand Faces*[2] Joseph Campbell gives a clear account of its sources and appearances. He describes the various phases of the heroic journey as a traditional monomyth.

In the myth there are usually three dominant movements which are cyclic in pattern. They are the departure of the hero, the initiation, and the return from his heroic adventure. It cannot be dogmatically stated that all heroes in fiction will follow the precise and stereotyped pattern of the heroic journey down to the last detail, but most follow some aspect of at least one of the categories described by Campbell. All of the stages need not be present, nor is it the nature of the journey to allow easy completion. Many works illustrate the initial refusal of the call to adventure, while others depict protagonists who cannot overcome the obstacles along the way. There are also accounts of those heroes who have undertaken the journey and surmounted all obstacles but refuse to return to society with the light gained as a result of the adventure. Whenever the hero does proceed through all the stages, a more coherent and complete design is effected at the narrative level. What is more important is that as the completion of the journey attests to a unity of thematic purpose on the underlying psychological and mythic level, it also depicts the fulfillment of the process of individuation.

How much of Hemingway's use of the journey artifice and other manifestations of psychological and mythological symbolism is conscious or unconscious is, of course, difficult if not impossible to ascertain. Certain assumptions may be made as to the sources of his material, however, no matter what its level of conscious utilization. Principally, as a modern man living in the twentieth century, Hemingway would have available all of the materials from the traditional sources of the culture. This cultural inheritance alone can account for his knowledge of the journey pattern. Whether he adapted it consciously or intuitively, he almost certainly observed it in his reading.

As Campbell's description of the heroic journey as a monomyth indicates, the motif has a variety of sources in the literatures of many nations, both ancient and modern. The Fisher King and Grail myths provide some of the earliest sources for these patterns. In *From Ritual to Romance* Jesse Weston cites an example of the quest motif in one of the early Fisher King stories, *Sone de Nansai:* "To sum up the result of the analysis . . . that the story postulates a close connection between the vitality of a certain King, and the prosperity of his kingdom; the forces of the ruler being weakened or destroyed, by wound, sickness, old age, or death, the land becomes Waste, and the task of the hero is that of restoration." [3] Here are the basic aspects of the artifice, but the significance of the myth cannot be said to lie simply on the surface of the story structure;

rather, the myths are part of the universal psychic patterns of all mankind. Carl G. Jung has examined this relationship at length, and in a discussion of the poet's employment of myth, he says: "It is to be expected of the poet that he will resort to mythology in order to give his experience its most fitting expression. . . . The primordial experience is the source of his creativeness; it cannot be fathomed, and therefore requires mythological imagery to give it form." [4]

Many more examples of hero myths can be found than those in the early Grail and Fisher King stories. Greek and Roman literature abound with them and supply some outstanding citations. For example, Jason's quest for the Golden Fleece represents an illuminating illustration of the traditional journey. The many trials and obstacles he is forced to overcome closely parallel the initiation rites that the Grail heroes must perform in their quest. In the Theseus story the escape from the Labyrinth after slaying the Minotaur furnishes a classic basis for the description of all subsequent symbolic journeys. From this myth emerge the important images of the labyrinth, the psychic chaos from which all men must escape in order to obtain selfhood, and the Minotaur, the psychic monster or other self which must be defeated within the confines of a labyrinthian unconscious world.

Vergil's hero, Aeneas, must take his ritual journey into the underworld. There he must cross the threshold of the river of the dead and pass by the ogre figure of the three-headed watchdog, Cerberus, in order to talk with the ghost of his father. The boon for the hero is the revelation of future events and an insight into methods of avoiding pain in the world. He returns from the underworld and crosses the return threshold of the "ivory gate," thus having symbolically attained selfhood. In *The Divine Comedy* of Dante the journey is similar to that in the *Aeneid*. Dante must also cross the threshold of life and pursue his quest through the underworld with Vergil as his guide. This situation presents another figure in the traditional journey, the classic guide. This all-important personage either leads the hero or points the way toward the quest. Usually the guide has some special aptitude for this function, such as having completed his own journey, as Vergil has symbolically taken such a journey before Dante. A further characteristic of the guide is his supernatural power, whether given by some deity, as in the case of Vergil in *The Divine Comedy,* or given by Satan, as in the case of Mephistopheles in the Faust legends.

The richest and most influential source of myth available to all artists in Western culture is the Bible. Here there is an abundance of allegorical and symbolical stories of heroic journeys, from the Noah story in Genesis, through the great exodus of the Hebrew nation led by Moses, into the New Testament with the Christ story, and ending with the mystic crossing from the conscious world into the visionary world by St. John the Divine. All of these stories contain the essential elements of the symbolic journey, and they all contain the same thematic patterns that occur in other myths of the hero.

These recurring patterns appear in many ancient and modern works, and their complex meanings are often difficult to interpret. The most enlightening comments in this connection have come from Jung, and his is one of the major influences on that branch of literary criticism which has emphasized the use of psychological, mythological, and anthropological materials.

By using these materials at least two broad areas of interpretation and movement in all works of art may be recognized: the surface level, or outward movement, with the literal development of plot; and the psychological level, or inner movement, incorporating imagery and symbol as the primary means of expression. In Hemingway's works the employment of the journey artifice provides an outstanding example of these two movements. In his use of the artifice one can discern the employment of a surface narrative technique as his simple, mechanical method of furthering plot development, but one can just as surely discover that the content of his novels and stories, the more meaningful revelation, is far below the surface and lies in the realm of symbolic allusion. In part, the high artistry of Hemingway's fiction is derived from his ability to utilize these levels of meaning in such a way as to fuse the content of a work with its form.

Chapter III

Initiation Experiences

THROUGHOUT HEMINGWAY'S FICTION there is a vital concern with the roles that people are expected to play in the central drama of life. This concern manifests itself in the short stories which deal with the hero as a young boy. Principally it operates in what may be termed as an expectancy versus fulfillment complex. That is, individuals have certain notions derived from social customs and conventions about the way particularly important personages (parents, adults, the opposite sex) associated with their lives ought to act and what they ought to be. Sometimes individuals measure up to the roles expected of them; most of the time they do not and cannot. Hemingway's adolescents and young men are particularly sensitive on this point. When these human models or exemplars fail to fulfill the expected role, the result is an intense inner conflict within the immature hero. The resolution of this conflict provides the dynamics of the adjustment process in the journey toward maturity.

In real-life situations the pattern of development is such that the result of insight may be disillusionment. This mood may be temporary or it may be permanent, depending upon the particular circumstances of the individual involved. For those who remain fixed at this point the goal of self-discovery is thwarted before the development has substantially begun. For those who glimpse the disillusionment implied by a learning situation and elect to avoid it by reverting to infantile fantasy where such knowledge is unknown, the end result is either fixation at that level or postponement of the inevitable. The complexities of the world and the nature of experience rarely allow the sensitive individual to remain secluded in infantilism for long, however, and willingly or unwillingly the individual is eventually thrust into the world of experience and forced to deal with it. If the individual is willing to accept the lessons of experience and adapt himself to contingencies over which he has little control, he can arrive ultimately at the apotheosis of the journey through experience and achieve the goal of individuation. If he cannot accept reality as it exists and remains fixed at some lesser level, he becomes a victim of his own disorientation, and alienation from the processes of life around him follows.

The development of an individual begins in the nursery, where he receives his earliest impressions of an external world. At this stage he receives a lasting impression of the central figures who are to care for him and guide him through the helpless stage into eventual maturity. These figures are the mother and father, and the early impressions of them reflect the extent of an individual's experience with two basic archetypal constructs. These are in their broader sense the mother and father images, and it is the vital experience with them that an individual carries throughout life. On one level an individual thereafter seeks to collate and adjust to his initial experience in the cradle all future encounters with the personifications of these mother and father archetypes—girl friend, mistress, wife, on the one hand, and wise old man, healer, and hero figures of all varieties on the other.

One can only guess the extent of Hemingway's knowledge and interest in analytical psychology as a discipline, but a study of his treatment of a young boy as the central character in a number of his short stories illustrates that underlying his artistry there is a perceptive understanding of the development of the human mind. Taking a character at an early age, he depicts the first insights into a world of experience. Many times these insights are not pleasant for the character, and many times he refuses to accept as real what he has viewed. At other times the character will make some minor adjustment to the experience which may not seem apparent on the literal level. At any event, throughout the sequence of short stories treating the young hero, Hemingway constellates the primal conflicts which all men through all ages have experienced. As such, these stories illustrate Hemingway's concern with and exploration of the elemental inquiry concerning man's relationship to the cosmos.

When Hemingway gave the hero of so many of his early stories the name of "Nick Adams," he was doing more than designating a simple appellation to stand for a character. Rather, he intentionally used a symbolic name as a conscious device to illustrate what the character himself would reveal throughout every story in which he appeared. Yet the employment of such a device is not as simple and surface as it may seem at first glance, for Hemingway is too much of the artist to resort to the use of an unsophisticated allegoric device in its most obvious form. Once viewed in relation to the thematic content of the stories, the naming of the hero may be seen as full-blown charactery taken to its furthest implication.

The surname is particularly appropriate inasmuch as Nick Adams is in a very real sense a second Adam. He is not in any literal sense the progenitor of a whole race, but he does typify a whole race of contemporary men who have encountered irrational elements in their environment and have been forced to deal with them. In the stories in which Nick is depicted as a young boy, he is the innocent, akin to the first Adam before the Fall. But as in the biblical story, the state of innocence is short-lived, and the serpent here too enters the "garden." In this case, however, the entry is not a blatant caricature of the forces of evil; it is the subtle growing of awareness of the incalculable events that disturb the natural order of things, of the caprice in that disturbance, and, what is more important, it is a growing of awareness of the irrational forces that operate within the self.

Hemingway directly reinforces the implications of the name "Adam" as incorporating the forces of evil and the chthonic by giving his hero a first name that might easily be associated with "Old Nick" or Satan, the archetype of evil. Having thus named his character, Hemingway in one stroke characterizes the inherited tendencies of all men. The tension created by the implications of the association of these names is in itself archetypal in its suggestion of the eternal struggle between the forces of good and evil. But the hero in the Hemingway stories encounters evil in many guises, and it goes by many names, be it a wound—literal or psychological—terror in the night, death, or anything else. Always, however, evil is inescapable and unpredictable. In many ways what the Hemingway hero must learn throughout the stories is the nature of evil, and the tension created by the struggle of opposing forces within himself provides the underlying dynamics for the learning process.

Experience itself may be one of the guises of contingent evil. Just as surely as eating the fruit of the tree of knowledge precipitated Adam's fall, so for the innocent the initial encounter with elements foreign to the womb-like existence of home and mother is the first stage of a long and dangerous journey. To the individual involved, retreat from the implications of this first encounter might seem possible, but once exposed, his own nature automatically commits him to the entire journey. If he denies the validity of the commitment, he merely postpones the inevitable or damns himself eternally to the regions of infantile fantasy.

In the short story "Indian Camp," the first of the "Nick" stories of *In Our Time,* Hemingway illustrates the compelling tendency to revert to the state of naïve innocence once the first contact with forces outside the protected environment has been made. Nick as a young boy accompanies his father, a doctor, to an Indian village where an Indian woman is to have a baby. Traveling with Nick and his father is Uncle George, who becomes a register against which the attitudes of Nick's father may be tested. The story evolves out of the central incident in which the baby is delivered by Caesarean section. Certain revelations concerning the doctor's character emerge because of the method of delivery, for he has failed to bring along the proper equipment. The operation must be performed with a jack-knife and without benefit of an anesthetic. As a result of the woman's screams during the operation, her husband, who has been lying all the while in the overhead bunk with a severe ax wound, commits suicide by cutting his throat.

Although the surface plot is of some consequence in itself, the major focus of the story is Nick's reaction to these events. This emphasis clarifies in light of the initiatory motif around which the story is constructed, and a seemingly slight interlude with a bizarre ending is revealed as having more than situational import. In this story Hemingway establishes a controlling symbol, the Indian camp itself. As in other stories, the camp is suggestive of the primitive and dark side of life. It is a manifestation of the intrusive and irrational elements that impose upon the secure and rational faculties where order and light prevail. For Nick, whose own home is across the lake, the night journey to the camp has all the possibilities of a learning experience. But he must be prepared to accept the knowledge it can give him. As it turns out, Nick is incapable of accepting the events he has witnessed, and the initial preview of the realities of the world is abortive.

Hemingway prepares the reader for Nick's encounter with the dark forces by employing details of setting suggestive of the mysterious and other-worldly: "The two boats started off in the dark. Nick heard the oarlocks of the other boat quite a way ahead of them in the mist. The Indians rowed with quick choppy strokes. Nick lay back with his father's arm around him. It was cold on the water" (91). The classical parallel is too obvious to overlook, for the two Indians function in a Charon-like fashion in transporting Nick, his father, and his uncle from their own sophisticated and civilized world of the white man into the dark and primitive world of the camp. Hemingway also invokes a conscious contrast in his use of another classical device, the guide figure. Here, the father takes Nick along to the camp, and he protectively has his arm around Nick. In the passage that follows, it is to his father that Nick directs the meaningful question, another traditional device of the journey artifice: "Where are we going, Dad?" The answer his father gives is indicative of the protective parental mantle that refuses to allow the child to face directly certain adult terrors. Rather than tell Nick outright, the father-guide here attempts to diminish the import of the coming event: "Over to the Indian camp. There is an Indian lady very sick" (91).

The father as guide figure for the son is to this point of the story a portrait of a natural and harmonious relationship. Yet Hemingway has imposed the figures of the two Indians and Uncle George almost in thumbnail sketch, and their function is important in the symbolic equation that is the basic form of the story. In crossing the lake to the dark side, the Indians control the movement, and Uncle George rides in the lead boat. He smokes a cigar and gives cigars to the two Indians, reminiscent of the smoking ritual and symbolizing unity and harmony with the forces represented by the Indians. Later, Uncle George becomes emotional over the events of the delivery, signaling his further involvement. Finally, it is Uncle George's telling comment which points out the ineptitude of the father as a man of science and representative of a rational and civilized world in his dealings with dark forces that lie outside his province. This commentary occurs after the operation when, as the narrator relates, the doctor "was feeling exalted and talkative as football players are in the dressing room after a game." He then addresses Uncle George: " 'That's one for the medical journal, George,' he said. 'Doing a Caesarean with a jack-knife and sewing it up with nine-foot, tapered gut leaders.' " With telling irony Uncle George reveals all the inadequacies of the doctor in his naïve attempt to impose order in a world of disorder. He tells the doctor, " 'Oh, you're a great man, all right' " (94).

That the father as a man has not himself come to terms with the irrational and uncontrollable forces at work is made obvious by his reaction to the suicide of the Indian husband. When the delivery of the child apparently is going well, the father—in the guise of doctor-scientist—gives Nick a step-by-step account of its progress. At one point he even tells Nick that the screams of the woman are not important. But the statement is ironic, for the husband commits suicide because of the screams. When the doctor discovers the death of the Indian, his control of the situation is lost. He is left with "all his post-operative exhilaration gone." He tells Nick, " 'it was an awful mess to put you through' " (94). In this way the studied control of the father as doctor and rational man disintegrates, and all that is left is father as fallible man. In effect, the father has been stripped of his own protective mask, the doctor-scientist *persona*, and he is forced to deal with the situation as a man with an unmasked ego.

Hemingway has further imposed a significant aspect of the theme of individuation. That is, the hero is constantly forced to adjust in some manner to the prime manifestations of the irrational: pain and death in the world. The two father figures here, the doctor and the "wounded" Indian, are in apposition to each other, but each reacts in a different way. Both are equally ineffectual, however, and this fact illustrates their denial of that role. The Indian as a primitive has no effective method of dealing with the terror created by the screaming wife. On the other hand, as long as Nick's father is in the role of doctor and performs the rituals assigned to the healer, he assumes he can cope with and control the forces of life and death. When the Indian by his suicide denies his role and function as father and husband, the doctor's role as healer is at the same time put in a ridiculous light. Thus Hemingway illustrates the absurdity of man, in any guise, in his attempt to control forces which are not in his power.

The figure of Uncle George as a foil to the doctor is further exhibited in relation to the guise of the father as healer and man of science. During the delivery, when the doctor apparently has the situation under complete control, Uncle George is bitten by the woman while trying to hold her down. His response, "Damn squaw bitch," an emotional and uncontrolled one, signifies his ability to respond naturally to pain. The doctor, in that role, affects an air of detachment in direct opposition to the responses of the uncle. With the suicide the obvious point of the unreality of such a pose is made.

When his father fails to sustain the expected role, Nick reverts to infantile dependence. At the end of the story the pair row back to the other side of the lake, and Nick questions his father about the implications of the events of the night. Nick's denial of the learning experience begins when he addresses his father as "Daddy" instead of "Dad," as he had at the beginning. But the most telling revelation of the abortive nature of the learning situation comes when he asks, " 'Is dying hard, Daddy?' " Having witnessed the bizarre events at the camp, the question reflects his inability to grasp the significance of his exposure to pain and death. Further, by slipping back into the role of the inexperienced one Nick thus effects a reconstruction of the father. Both the denial of the experience—or admission of his insensitivity to it—and the attempt to recreate the father as man into the infantile father-*imago* likeness are sublimated at this point.

Nick's refusal to accept the terrors of pain and death and the father's inability to cope with them are revealed in an ironic light in the conclusion: "In the early morning on the lake sitting in the stern of the boat with his father rowing, he [Nick] felt quite sure that he would never die" (95). But Nick has been exposed to some of the primal terrors of human experience, and his "feeling" is depicted as illusory and child-like because it is a romantic reaction to the experience he has undergone. The irony enters in the portrait of the young Nick "sitting in the stern," implying that he is in control of the boat—events; yet it is the father who rows, and he has already proven ineffectual for such a role. The details of setting further point up the irony, for "the sun was coming up over the hills." In contrast with the events of the night the sun may seem to dispel darkness, but at the same time it foreshadows the coming of night again.

In "The Doctor and the Doctor's Wife," the second of the "Nick" stories of *In Our Time*, the controlling symbol is once again the Indian camp. Here, however, instead of a journey to the camp, with all of the attendant psychological implications of such a journey, representatives of the camp are summoned across the lake to participate in the sophisticated and civilized world of Nick and his father. The locale is northern Michigan, and the fact that it is the edge of a wilderness gives the setting a significance beyond a mere backdrop. This is a border zone area, symbolically a meeting place of two opposing forces, and here Nick as the young inexperienced one will undergo the initiatory rites which eventually project him into the role of young manhood. This site is the ground of home and parental protection, and the eventual severance from this influence must be won. These functions are not separate and distinct, for on the journey toward individuation the encounter with the dark powers can come only after a complete detachment from all of the infantile regressive tendencies has been accomplished.

Nick as yet is unequipped to undertake the complete journey, but the repeated experience with stark reality and the cumulative effects of such experience eventually project him into the greater effort. In "The Doctor and the Doctor's Wife," as the title reveals, the surface conflict involves two important personages in Nick's life and posits the two diverging axes of the archetypal nursery drama. The central conflict that emerges reveals a further step in the learning process that Nick undergoes in the story sequence of which this is a part.

[The plot concerns a short altercation that takes place between Nick's father and Dick Boulton, a half-breed from the Indian camp, over whether or not some beech logs washed ashore from a log boom are to be regarded as stolen, as Boulton contends, or as driftwood, as Nick's father assumes. A moral question is posed, although no one knows whether the steamer crew will return to claim the logs. After Boulton, his son, and another Indian leave without cutting the logs for the doctor, the original purpose for which they had come, the doctor with some restraint tells his wife of the argument and then leaves to go hunting with Nick.

As a half-breed, Dick Boulton incorporates the features and powers of both the white man and the Indian, symbolically the light and the dark, the known and unknown. He is a border zone figure and has available knowledge that is denied those who are committed to one or the other of the opposing regions. Through him Hemingway creates a tension of the opposites. Boulton is the exemplar who stands in rebellion against the authority of Nick's father. The encounter between the two undermines Nick's trust in his father, making the need to search for other authority figures the more urgent. Nick is by no means capable of beginning an active quest at this stage of his development, nor does Hemingway intend an obvious rebellion on Nick's part. Boulton is the revelator, and the accumulation of such encounters will later convince Nick that authority at any level is spurious.

⌐The ringing irony of Boulton's appearance in the story is that the doctor himself summons this figure from out of the dark land of the Indian camp. In this way the doctor contributes to his own downfall in the eyes of his son. Hemingway intensifies the irony of the situation by interposing the moral question of whether or not the logs are stolen. As a representative of the society of which Nick will become a part, and as a supporter of the ethical code to which that society adheres, the doctor is defeated on a question of moral import by a representative of a supposed lower and more primitive level of culture. Thus, not only is the father figure denigrated in Nick's eyes, but also the moral framework of Nick's entire society is undermined.⌐

The argument scene with Boulton is not the central focus of the story, but it does serve as the catalyst for the ensuing albeit inapparent nursery drama. This drama as such implies the triadic conflict of the child versus both parents in his desire to free himself from parental domination and achieve autonomy. Hemingway depicts the effects of this conflict in the second and in the final scenes of the story.

In the second scene Hemingway emphasizes the conflict and points up the breech between the two parents by injecting an additional irony. The father as doctor, scientist, or representative of the rational order of things is juxtaposed to the mother, a Christian Scientist. The irony in the utter divergence of thought between the two is brought into sharp focus when the doctor returns to the house and tersely tells his wife that he has had a row with Boulton.

> "Oh," said his wife, "I hope you didn't lose your temper, Henry."
>
> "No," said the doctor.
>
> "Remember, that he who ruleth his spirit is greater than he that taketh a city," said his wife. She was a Christian Scientist. Her Bible, her copy of *Science and Health* and her *Quarterly* were on a table beside her bed in the darkened room.
>
> Her husband did not answer. He was sitting on his bed now, cleaning a shotgun. He pushed the magazine full of the heavy yellow shells and pumped them out again. They were scattered on the bed. (101-02)

Other than the obvious irony of a physician's wife belonging to a religious sect which denies the necessity of his professional function, there are several other levels of consideration here. The reason for the mother's lying in a darkened room in broad daylight is not given, but the implication is that she is ill, a fact which further heightens the surface irony. Whether or not this is so, however, the detail serves to illustrate that she is ineffectual in her role as wife and mother and even as a social entity. As mother-preserver and protectress of the innocent, she is portrayed here symbolically as languishing in the womb-like province of her darkened room. As such, she is at once the fatal or terrible mother figure who would lure her son back to the womb to be smothered by her protective nature. Thus she would destroy any possibility of the son ever reaching the goal of self-realization. In classical literature this feature of the mother archetype is often depicted by the sirens who lure sailors from their natural course. The results there are identical with the psychological implications of this situation: for those who succumb to the call, death or regression is the inevitable result. The mother, like Circe who would turn men into swine, represents a romantic refusal to accept the realities of life. When the doctor tells her he believes Boulton started the argument to avoid paying a bill, she responds unrealistically: " 'Dear, I don't think, I really don't think anyone would really do a thing like that' " (102). The lure of this wooing mother figure provides one axis — the romance of escape to the womb — of the underlying conflict inherent in the nursery drama.

Hemingway distinctly delineates the abode of the mother and the region of the father by drawing attention to the psychological schism with particular, literal details and by symbolic allusion. After the conversation between the mother and father in which it becomes obvious that they are at odds, the narrator relates: "The doctor went out on the porch. The screen door slammed behind him. He heard his wife catch her breath when the door slammed. 'Sorry,' he said, outside her window with the blinds drawn. 'It's all right dear,' she said" (102-03). The flat, inexpressive quality implied by the tone of the dialogue suggests in itself that all is not "all right" between the doctor and his wife. The fact that the doctor is "outside her window with the blinds drawn" illustrates symbolically the alienation of the father from the womb, and consequently reflects the mother-son-father triadic conflict. Thus the divergency of the two positions demonstrates dramatically the attractions which test Nick's ability to select his own course of life. Since the role of the father is to provide the impetus for the son's projection beyond the protective presence of the womb, Nick's selection must be that which will somehow come to terms with the father.

Nick's direct involvement in this interlude is first apparent when the mother tells the doctor, " 'If you see Nick, dear, will you tell him his mother wants to see him?' " (102). The fact that Hemingway has her refer to herself in the third person immediately suggests a peculiarity in her personality and perhaps a more serious psychological aberration. In effect, referring to herself as a separate entity from the "I" which is speaking accomplishes a depersonalization of her ego, a further illustration of her complete separation from the world of reality.

Nick's task is to escape from this temptress who threatens his development into maturity, and he does. At the end of the story with his denial of her, she becomes the image of frustration and unrelatedness, wasting away in isolation and solitude. Hemingway thus correlates her role as temptress-mother with her religious affiliation, neither of which is depicted as valid for the hero in his epic struggle.

For Nick, standing on the threshold of adolescence and as yet unable to make any significant break from parental domination, the possibilities of reconciling what he has witnessed seem small. Yet in the final scene he does come to terms with the situation. Finding Nick sitting under a tree, reading — an escape — the father tells him: " 'Your mother wants you to come and see her.' " But Nick rejects, " 'I want to go with you,' " and takes the first step by denying escape through mother and reconstructing the father image. There is a tinge of irony, though, for in the exchange that follows Nick is at once deferential ("Daddy") and at the same time commanding: " 'I know where there's black squirrels, Daddy,' Nick said. 'All right,' said his father. 'Let's go there' " (103). By this means Hemingway illustrates the effect of the total experience upon Nick. In a sense Nick has usurped the function of the father in his attempt to reconstruct him. Now it is Nick who is to be the guide, and significantly it is to the woods that they are to go. Symbolically, the journey is toward experience, not retreat to the womb of mother. This is in effect a completion of the symbolic equation posited at the beginning of the story where Boulton precipitated the adventure for Nick. The woods are illustrative of the dark qualities represented by the Indian, and it is into the woods that Nick is to lead the fallible father figure in order to restore him.

These early stories preface to a considerable extent many of the activities in which the hero of the later ones will engage. Whether he is in the guise of Nick Adams—the new Adam—or under some other apellation, the hero must learn to adjust to contingencies, reconcile himself to them, and eventually create for himself a new moral center in harmony with his own innermost drives. As both of these early stories illustrate, the tremendous task of self-discovery requires the loss of all former attachments that indicate infantile dependence. As the hero divests himself of all former ideals, the creation of a new self must follow.

The Hemingway hero learns the difficulty of this task, as all heroes in literature have learned before him.

In "Indian Camp" and in "The Doctor and the Doctor's Wife," Nick is depicted as a young boy on the threshold of adolescence. His actions and responses are unemotive and childlike. He reacts rather than acts in a given situation, and his initiatory experiences border a *via negativa*. This is typical of the young innocent about to begin the greater journey, but that journey is one that requires a positive commitment to an essentially moral purpose.

In the third story of the Nick sequence the title serves as a rubric to the surface plot as well as to the underlying psychological level of the story. "The End of Something" as a title indicates that this is to be a story of termination; it also poses a question as to the nature of the "Something."

The plot concerns Nick and a girl friend, Marjorie, and relates the events of a night fishing trip the two have taken. Nick has apparently planned in advance that this is to be the finale of their romantic interlude, for after preparing for the night's fishing and making the camp he tells Marjorie that "it isn't fun anymore." Marjorie leaves him, terminating the affair, and Nick's friend arrives as part of the prearranged plan. The story closes with a touch of irony, for Nick is unhappy with the outcome of the episode.

> "Did she go all right?" Bill said.
> "Yes," Nick said, lying, his face on the blanket.
> "Have a scene?"
> "No, there wasn't any scene."

"How do you feel?"

"Oh, go away, Bill! Go away for a while."

Bill selected a sandwich from the lunch basket and walked over to have a look at the rods. (111)

In the final portion of this story a definite progression has been accomplished in the development of Nick Adams from child to adolescent, for with the exhibition of his inner feelings he has at the same time revealed his sensibility. No longer is he girded in the armor of protective infantile illusion and detachment; he takes a positive course of action, and he alone must bear the brunt of its consequences. The "Something" that has come to an end is his belief in the efficacy of romantic illusion. Hemingway evolves a situation in which the landscape becomes the overriding symbol which points to the termination of an old habit of mind.

The pattern which Hemingway chose to depict Nick's emotive display of sensibility as a step toward learning is in itself a significant illustration of his artistry. Initially he prefaces the actual story involving Nick with a correlative parable of exploitation and waste that, in an emblematic fashion, foreshadows the whole of the coming story.

In the old days Hortons Bay was a lumbering town. No one who lived in it was out of sound of the big saws in the mill by the lake. Then one year there were no more logs to make lumber. The lumber schooners came into the bay and were loaded with the cut of the mill that stood stacked in the yard. All the piles of lumber were carried away. The big mill building had all its machinery that was removable taken out and hoisted on board one of the schooners by the men who had worked in the mill. The schooner moved out of the bay toward the open lake carrying the two great saws, the travelling carriage that hurled the logs against the revolving, circular saws and all the rollers, wheels, belts and iron piled on a hull-deep load of lumber. Its open hold covered with canvas and lashed tight, the sails of the schooner filled and it moved out into the open lake, carrying with it everything that had made the mill a mill and Hortons Bay a town. (107)

This initial vignette prefigures Nick's coming separation from Marjorie. The exception is that as a man Nick cannot so easily escape the consequences of his acts as could the lumber company. The use of the traditional story-of-the-land device serves both as emblem and as a simple method of establishing the mood of the story.

As the story unfolds, the significance of the appended parable and its relation to the dominant motif of the cycle of existence becomes apparent. We are told that "ten years later there was nothing of the mill left except broken white limestone of its foundations showing through the swampy second growth as Nick and Marjorie rowed along the shore" (107). The image of "second growth" is repeated throughout the story. As a collective image it manifests a symbolic reflection of the pair of young lovers. They too are second growth, as it were, and they are participants in the great cycle of existence. As the emblem of the story indicates, the cycle implies a death and waste in the existing order of things before a renewal may occur. Nick's growing of awareness is equated with the loss of the mill. The taking away of the vital machinery that "made the mill a mill" symbolizes Nick's loss of belief in the ordered machinations of his childish universe. The loss he is to suffer is parallel to the loss of the town. Only the marks upon his sensibility will remain, just as the only sign of the mill and town that remain are the marks upon the countryside.

Marjorie is unaware of the awakening of consciousness in Nick, and her responses reveal the pattern of Nick's inner attitudes. As they pass points in the landscape which to her are indicative of the romance of life, Nick views them in the light of his newly found sensibility. She sees the remnants of the mill as "our old ruin," or later, "a castle." Nick either gives a matter-of-fact reply or does not answer to these words steeped in emotion. When he tells her, " 'It isn't fun anymore,' " Marjorie still clings to the illusion: " 'Isn't love any fun?' " Nick's response seemingly reflects an adolescent inability to articulate his inner feelings, but the irony of the term "fun" is apparent. Nick as child-initiate is ego-centered and he must free himself from this attitude in order to participate in the activities of an adult world. When Nick displays his hurt over the separation from Marjorie in the conclusion, he at the same time indicates the lesson that the experience has taught him: it isn't any fun *without* Marjorie, either. Hemingway so constructs the plot that the conclusion reflects back to the correlative parable in the introduction. Nick cannot neatly pack everything up and sail off onto the lake as the schooner had done, for the experience has left an emotional scar. ⌐

The awakening of Nick's sensibility in this story and his learning that emotional attachments are not easily severed foreshadows the thin-skinned sensitivity to hurt that the later heroes exhibit. Every myth of the hero begins with these calls to adventure, be they a precise herald figure, vague yearnings within the individual, or simply emotional crises. Regardless of the mode in which the call manifests itself, however, the pre-journey conditions are present and provide the apparent motivation for the hero figure. Always behind the surface circumstance lies the inward sphere of the hero's consciousness where a moral conflict must stir, and the outward circumstances serve as a catalyst to activate the hero's desire for the quest. In these early stories, when the young Nick is emotionally disturbed by his treatment of another individual, the first stirrings of a moral sense arise within him.

"The Three-Day Blow" is the fourth in the sequence, and it expands the characterization of Nick. In this story Hemingway depicts a boastful, adolescent central character. His actions and attitudes, however, re-enforce the importance of the initiation into life encountered in "Indian Camp," the destruction of the father figure in "The Doctor and the Doctor's Wife," and the insight gained into the cycle of existence in "The End of Something." The story may be said to be a story of recapitulation.

The subject matter directly complements "The End of Something." The events take place not long after those depicted in the earlier story and illustrate Nick's reactions. Essentially an adjustment story, it relates Nick's coming to Bill's cabin and talking of baseball, literature, and his affair with Marjorie. At the conclusion, having first decided to get drunk, then having decided not to get drunk, they go out to find Bill's father and to hunt. The surface line of action is obviously scant, but that is of little significance. What is important is the revelation of Nick's attitudes toward his experiences and toward life in general.

At the psychological level something quite different is expressed from what at first glance seems obvious at the literal level. Nick here engages in a fantasy of infantile regression and escape within that regression. This tendency is not unusual in any journey toward discovery of the self, for the implications of experience with the forces beyond the control of the individual are terrifying. No one would choose to destroy himself — an act which is what the discovery of the self implies — unless under the severest provocation. Thus it is that all heroes who set out on this journey have at some point faltered on the way. Nick Adams is no exception.

In the opening of the story Hemingway resorts to an expressionistic device in order to externalize the inner attitudes of his central character. It is autumn, the fruit has been picked, and the wind is blowing through bare trees. Nick picks up a fallen apple "shiny in the brown grass from the rain." Next he views the idyllic scene into which he is to retreat: "The road came out of the orchard on the top of the hill. There was the cottage, the porch bare, smoke coming from the chimney. In back was the garage, the chicken coop and the second growth timber like a hedge against the woods behind." Still, reflected against this idyll are signs and portents of nature which point to something other than retreat from inner disturbances over the Marjorie affair: "The big trees swayed far over in the wind as he watched. It was the first of the autumn storms" (115). Nature itself indicates that severance, though it may be transient — as are the seasons of nature — is also cyclic. For Nick, if he could translate these omens, the implication would be clear: the episode with Marjorie is only one of many coming hurts that as a man and part of this cycle he will have to undergo.

Another factor of importance to the psychology of Nick's development is his turning to a number of escape mechanisms to compensate for the inner frustrations created by his severance from Marjorie. With Bill he indulges in "sophisticated" adult talk. Throughout this exchange it is apparent that Nick has progressed to a level of maturity beyond that of Bill. Nick has experienced an emotional hurt, and he exhibits the knowledge he has gained because of it. When they are discussing a book called *Forest Lovers*, an obviously romantic and sentimental piece, Bill suggests that it is a good book. Nick, on the other hand, in a passage reminiscent of Huck's attitude toward Tom Sawyer's pirate books in *Adventures of Huckleberry Finn*, evinces a more realistic attitude:

> "What else have you got I haven't read?" Nick asked.
> "Did you ever read the *Forest Lovers?*"
> "Yup. That's the one where they go to bed every night with the naked sword between them."
> "That's a good book, Wemedge."

"It's a swell book. What I couldn't ever understand was what good the sword would do.
It would have to stay edge up all the time because if it went over flat you could roll right
over it and it wouldn't make any trouble."

"It's a symbol," Bill said.

"Sure," said Nick, "but it isn't practical." (118)

Bill's reference to Nick as "Wemedge" reflects the
typical adolescent posture in its attempt to appear
"sophisticated." Rather than depicting poise, however,
it pointedly illustrates an adolescent habit of mind.
Nick's "practical" bent, on the other hand, portrays
an awakened mode of thought.

The pivotal point in the narrative comes when
the conversation turns to Marjorie.

"All of a sudden it was over," Nick said. "I
oughtn't to talk about it."

"You aren't," Bill said. "I talked about it
and now I'm through. We won't ever speak
about it again. You don't want to think about
it. You might get back into it again."

Nick had not thought about that. It had
seemed so absolute. That was a thought. That
made him feel better.

"Sure," he said. "There's always that
danger."

He felt happy now. There was not anything
that was irrevocable. He might go into town
Saturday night. Today was Thursday.

"There's always the chance," he said. (124)

Here Hemingway concisely telescopes the optimism
that a youthful hero may hold. To deny the positive

insight that a vital experience has provided is in effect to regress. When Nick thinks that "nothing was finished" and that "nothing was ever lost," he reverts to the infantile and illusory attitudes expressed in "Indian Camp" where he felt he could "live forever." This is not adjustment to the experience — a necessary step toward development; it is a direct denial of the implications of that experience. Poised on the threshold of illumination, Nick takes a step backward. He is not capable of crossing the threshold into more vital experiences as yet.

Having sidestepped the too dangerous movement forward in his own development toward maturity, Nick further exhibits the regressive tendencies invoked at the moment of crisis. He and Bill feel "swell," and they decide to seek the comfort of adolescent excitement by going out to hunt. They are not to go alone, however, for they are going to seek Bill's father. Nick in effect seeks the security of a surrogate father-hero — Bill's father — and once again turns to the comfort and security of the protective parental mantle.

Hemingway supports this type of interpretation by so imposing details of external nature that it is obvious they are complementary to the central theme of the story. Nick's belief that something can be undone — "You *can* go home again," to distort Wolfe's phrase — is a denial of the lesson nature teaches. Although the changes of external nature are cyclic and seem to indicate that spring is not far behind winter, to not realize that these are small cycles in the midst of a greater cosmic cycle of things where change is the very essence is to misinterpret. Nick here, too, is guilty, and in the end of the story he is poised at the peak of his infantile optimism: "None of it was important now. The wind blew it out of his head. Still he could always go into town Saturday night. It was a good thing to have in reserve" (125).

Hemingway apparently was keenly aware of and much interested in the inability of youth to accept the reality of a given situation. In all of these early stories, even though an external narrator relates the events, it is the youthful Nick's sensibility that is always the central focus. No doubt this was a conscious consideration on Hemingway's part in the construction of the stories, for the tone that dominates these narratives if not sympathetic at least is not one of condemnation. The stories deal with a segment of real-life experience. The hero's exposure to the variety of forces which operate in the world and over which he has no control point to Hemingway's concern with the relationship of all men to an external world not of their making. The fact that many of the stories are complementary to each other, as in the Nick sequence, illustrates not so much Hemingway's concern with one generic hero as his intense desire to explore the various psychological implications of the first, almost primal experiences with life.

Hemingway again deals with the subject of a young boy's initiation into life via his early attachments in "Ten Indians," a story which appeared in the collection *Men Without Women*. Although Nick, or "Nickie" as he is addressed by the other characters, is somewhat younger than in either "The End of Something" or "The Three-Day Blow," a dimension is added to the themes developed in the earlier pair.

The events which take place parallel to some extent those which the older Nick experiences, but here the loss of a "girl friend" is treated as a study in comic pathos. Nevertheless, with the unplanned dissolution of a childish affair, the reaction of this youthful Nick suggests a penetration into a deeper layer of emotional response.

At the outset Nick returns from town in a wagon with some neighbors. They have been to a Fourth of July celebration, and en route they have seen nine drunken Indians lying beside the road. When he arrives home, Nick is told by his father that while walking near the Indian camp he saw Nick's girl, Prudence Mitchell, an Indian girl, "threshing around" with another boy. Nick's reaction to this information is the point of the story.

The comic play of the "Ten Indians" in the title is apparent. Prudence is the tenth Indian, and the irony evolves from the derogatory remarks about Indians made by one of the boys during the ride home. Nick is also teased about the girl, but he "felt happy and hollow inside himself to be teased about Prudence Mitchell." Further irony is apparent in the girl's name, for she is anything but prudent. Also, her name is no more suggestive of her race than of her character. That it is the Fourth of July, Independence Day, being celebrated adds additional irony to the ending. It is Nick's day of independence, although a freedom of an unwanted sort comes to him.

The tone of this tale makes it impossible to interpret the "hurt" Nick receives from the affair in any fashion other than that it is bathetic. Hemingway pushes this bathos to the limit at the end of the story when Nick lies in bed and reflects: " 'My heart's broken,' he thought. 'If I feel this way my heart must be broken.' " In spite of the treatment, however, Hemingway still has a more serious point to make than mere parody of infantile suffering. In the final paragraph, the tone shifts and the story concludes on a note of seriousness.

> After a while he heard his father blow out the lamp and go into his own room. He heard a wind come up in the trees outside and felt it come in cool through the screen. He lay for a long time with his face in the pillow, and after a while he forgot to think about Prudence and finally he went to sleep. When he awoke in the night he heard the wind in the hemlock trees outside the cottage and the waves on the lake coming in on the shore, and he went back to sleep. In the morning there was a big wind blowing and the waves were running high up on the beach and he was awake a long time before he remembered that his heart was broken. (336)

Once again Hemingway resorts to images of nature in order to formulate by symbolic means a correlative in nature for the transformative or adaptive process taking place in his central character. Here, as in "The Three-Day Blow," a purificatory wind signals the cleansing and passing away of old hurts. Yet the wind is still part of a "storm," and the waves "running high" on the beach signal a coming psychological storm as well as a natural one. If Nick thinks that he has passed the crisis and that hurt has gone out of his life forever, he is belied in the final lines. Invoking an echo of the comic pathos sustained throughout the piece, Hemingway leaves no doubt of the transitory extent of Nick's "adaptation." When Nick is "awake a long time before he remembered that his heart was broken," he reflects a childish denial of the efficacy of the experience as a step towards maturation, but the recognition of the hurt is suggestive of the sensitivity he will have to other hurts in life.

Quite important in this story, as in all the early Nick stories, is the relationship between Nick and his father. The father directly confronts the hero with the bitter realities of the adult and mature world. Functioning in this fashion, the father performs his natural duty as guide for the infantile son who has been living in a world of childish romance. In that world everything is comic, in the broader sense of the term, but in the adult world one cannot escape from the hurts that are to come. The tenth Indian in this case is the one who forces home the consciousness of a dark world of uncertainty.

Nick's father in this story performs a further function which heightens the ambiguity of his role as a guide figure. He ministers to Nick's needs—feeds him—in a motherly fashion, but he also delivers the hurt. Thus Hemingway establishes one more facet of the complex of father images that appear throughout the short stories. The importance Hemingway gives this figure is not unexpected, for in any treatment of the themes of initiation and individuation the father is of central importance.

Once the process of maturation has begun it cannot be retarded for long, as Hemingway illustrates in a later story "Wine of Wyoming." There the son of Fontan, a Frenchman, worries about looking his age, for then he will have to pay for an adult ticket to the movie theater: " 'When I go to the show I crouch down like this and try to look small ' " (453). He is equally worried about gaining his manhood, and this is illustrated by his wish to hunt alone. He reads childish adventure books, signaling his inability to as yet complete the process of maturation: " 'I want to go all by myself and shoot all by myself. Next year I can do it.' He went over in a corner and sat down to read a book. I had picked it up when we came into the kitchen to sit after supper. It was a library book— *Frank on a Gunboat*" (456).

In "A Day's Wait," another of the later short stories which do not refer to Nick Adams, Hemingway depicts the father-son relationship in the coming-of-age cycle. The *tour de force* on which the plot hinges amply illustrates the suddenness of adaptation to the trauma of reality. The boy in this case has the name Schatz, and although seemingly made of sterner stuff he could still be a Nick Adams in his growing of awareness. In this story the boy is slightly ill with a fever, and, due to a confusion of the terms Fahrenheit and centigrade, he believes he is to die with a temperature of a hundred and two. For a full day he lives with this in mind, and the point of the story concerns itself with his reaction to this misconception.

In his belief that he is going to die, Schatz undergoes a complete transformation from child to adult. Hemingway illustrates this by an ironic reversal of roles. In the opening of the story, before Schatz finds out about his temperature, he resists going to bed in typical child-like fashion before finally submitting to the authority of his father. After he feels he is dying, however, he assumes the authoritarian role. When his father tries to read from a book of pirate stories, Schatz's normal fare, the boy does not listen. And when the father tells him to go to sleep, Schatz answers, "I'd rather stay awake." Finally he tells his father to leave the room, "if it's going to bother you." When the father goes hunting for a covey of quail, Hemingway does not depict him as an older person; rather, the father is portrayed more as a young boy thrilling to the adventure of the hunt. When he returns to the house after the hunt, Schatz forbids him to come into the room: " 'You can't come in,' he said. 'You mustn't get what I have' " (437-38).

The return to the normal role of child comes for Schatz when he learns of his error. The adult pose immediately drops and he reverts to his normal responses. Hemingway illustrates the change in this manner: "But his gaze at the foot of the bed relaxed slowly. The hold over himself relaxed too, finally, and the next day it was very slack and he cried very easily at little things that were of no importance" (439).

The adjustment to the inevitable and the heroic pose signal a different reaction to experience from that illustrated in the early Nick stories. Here, too, there is the regressive tendency, but it comes only after a victory over the inner forces of the self. It may be pointed out that this story is a later one and that Hemingway himself might have changed his own attitudes. Whatever the cause, a further dimension has been added to the story of the development of the Hemingway hero: personal inadequacies may be overcome in the face of pain and death.

In "God Rest You Merry, Gentlemen," Hemingway provides a contrasting view of Schatz's heroism. A young boy on the threshold of puberty asks the doctor to castrate him because of "the way he gets." The doctor cannot convince him that what is happening is part of a natural process. The boy gives his reasons: " 'It is wrong,' said the boy. 'It's a sin against purity. It's a sin against our Lord and Saviour' " (394). When the doctor absolutely refuses to castrate him, the boy leaves and mutilates himself with a razor. The refusal to accept the stage of puberty at which he has arrived is the extreme of the *via negativa*. But the analogy of sexual maturity with all of the processes of life and the eventual facing of death is made. The point is, all of Hemingway's boy-heroes do not accept contingencies as Schatz does in "A Day's Wait."

The early stirrings of sexuality also furnishes the material for one of the few stories which focus upon the sensibility of a female character. In "Up in Michigan" the central character is a young girl who is introduced to the sexual act. This experience with passion reveals the difficulties encountered on the threshold of adulthood and precipitates a sense of aloneness and isolation. Once her girlish notions of romance are reduced to mere animal experience, she is cast adrift into the adult world of contingency. After they have made love, her lover falls asleep in a drunken stupor. The narrative cites her reactions: "Liz leaned over and kissed him on the cheek. He was still asleep. She lifted his head a little and shook it. He rolled his head over and swallowed. Liz started to cry. She walked over to the edge of the dock and looked down to the water. There was a mist coming up from the bay. She was cold and miserable and everything felt gone" (85).

A still different facet of the coming of age theme is illustrated in "My Old Man." The plot is concerned with adjustment in the father-son relationship, and, in an echo of "The Doctor and the Doctor's Wife," it pivots on a question of moral import. In this story, even more than in the earlier story, the outcome is steeped in pathetic irony, and the hero is left on a plane of development from which there can be no return. One of the few places in which the young hero articulates his own plight, there is evident here a furthering of the theme of individuation beyond all of the stories involving the boy-hero.

The story is told in the first person with a boy, Joe, as narrator. By using this point of view, Hemingway is better able to exhibit the inner attitudes of the central character and reveal the pathos of the final learning situation. Further, the story is told in retrospect, which accounts for the tough, almost bitter tone of the piece. Such a tone intensifies the underlying conflicts of the story by illustrating the eventual attitude derived from the experiences. Thus Hemingway achieves a verisimilitude on two levels which enables him to project a moral beyond the isolated circumstances of a local situation in an individual story.

The opening lines foreshadow the coming disillusionment of the young boy with the father-hero. By the use of suggestive details, Hemingway coalesces the attitudes of the boy as narrator and the boy as participant in the action: "I guess looking at it, now, my old man was cut out for a fat guy, one of those regular little roly fat guys you see around, but he sure never got that way, except a little toward the last, and then it wasn't his fault, he was riding over the jumps only and he could afford to carry plenty of weight then" (191). The reference to the father by means of the familiar and almost pejorative expression "my old man" is indicative of a denigration of the father that has taken place since the time of the events of the story. It reflects as well the atmosphere in which the events have occurred. The reference to the father's physical characteristics, particularly his tendency to become fat, further alludes to his moral stature as depicted later in the story. The opening phrase, "I guess looking at it now," reveals the narrator's reluctance to admit the failure of the father and the consequent disillusionment, even though it is in retrospect that he is viewing the experience. The narrator's age is not given, but the assumption may be made that he is not yet of an age or level of development at which he is capable of reconciling the implications of such an admission.

The father in the story is a jockey in Europe, and the narrative reflects his stage-by-stage moral disintegration. This is paralleled on the literal level by his progressive inability to perform in his occupation. The structure of the story is such that the one becomes the symbolic equivalent of the other. Within the dramatic time of the story, there is an early foreshadowing of what is to come. The father must constantly run in a rubber suit in order to keep trim for riding, and he tells his son that it "is hell keeping it down." As the father begins to lose ground, physically and morally, he articulates his own plight in a metaphorical fashion: " 'This course rides itself. It's the pace you're going at that makes riding the jumps dangerous, Joe. We ain't going any pace here, and they ain't really bad jumps either. But it's the pace always — not the jumps — that makes the trouble' " (193).

The significance of the notion that it is the "pace" that ultimately defeats a man should not be understressed, for it is one which recurs in a myriad of ways in much of Hemingway's fiction. It is important, too, in any treatment of the underlying attitudes of the central characters in their quest for some sort of moral orientation in an unpredictable universe. In another short story called "A Pursuit Race," for example, Hemingway more precisely employs the metaphorical connotations of this notion by using it as a controlling device for the whole story. There the central character is the "advance-man" for a burlesque show, significantly enough, and must always stay ahead of the show. When he can no longer stand the "pace," symbolically the regimen of life, he allows the show to catch him and retreats to a womb-like existence of dope, liquor, and lying in his bed completely covered by a sheet. This act, of course, perfectly characterizes the negative way, and the same impulse to escape from life is manifested in a variety of ways by a host of other Hemingway characters.

The problem posed in "My Old Man" is of a similar order. The jockey-father is engaged in a "pursuit race" of his own, for he must keep ahead of the ominous "fat" which heralds old age and the subsequent loss of his means of existence. As he slowly loses ground, he cannot simply accept his fate. In a fashion reminiscent of "A Pursuit Race," where the central character tells his employer: " 'You're called

"Sliding Billy." That's because you can slide. I'm called just Billy. That's because I never could slide at all'" (353-54), the father does not "slide"—that is, adjust. Instead, he seeks to postpone the inevitable by involving himself in fixed races. This act is what finally destroys him as a hero figure.

For a young boy the approach to the realities of existence is of tremendous consequence, and the destruction of the infantile father-image is an ultimate necessity for his own progress. Hemingway depicts this destruction by the use of an underlying irony which summarily illustrates the tremendous void between infantile fantasy and the harsh world of adult reality. The process begins early in the narrative when Joe hears another man call his father a "son of a bitch." Until this time Joe has thought of his father as a strong figure who could face any kind of difficulty. Now he begins to find something wrong. "My old man sat there and sort of smiled at me, but his face was white and he looked sick as hell and I was scared and felt sick inside because I knew something had happened and I didn't see how anybody could call my old man a son of a bitch, and get away with it. My old man opened up the *Sportsman* and studied the handicaps for a while and then he said, 'You got to take a lot of things in this world, Joe'" (194).

What Joe has witnessed is fear in his father, and what becomes apparent later is that the father has become involved in something illegal and must leave the town. After leaving, their life is never the same. The father no longer can find work and he resorts to open illegality. It is not that the boy resents the illegal aspect of his father's livelihood but that the father has broken the trust placed in him as a hero in his profession. This altered status becomes apparent when Joe's father bets on a fixed race. Having been present when the jockey told his father what horse would win, Joe still does not totally grasp the implications of the situation. He romantically involves himself in the outcome of the race by attaching himself emotionally to the horse being ridden by the jockey who gave the tip. As expected, the horse loses. Still taken with the thrill of the race, the boy naïvely asks his father, " 'Wasn't it a swell race, Dad?' " The father, not realizing the extent of the childish involvement, answers, " 'George Gardner's a swell jockey, all right,' he said. 'It sure took a great jock to keep that Kzar horse from winning' " (200). The boy's reaction to this revelation is one of forced adjustment mingled with rationalization. He cannot at this point blame his father, for that would be to admit the fallibility of the father figure. The result of such an admission would be alienation and the resultant loss of the protection of the parental mantle. Nor does he reconstruct the father, as Nick did in an earlier story. Instead, he substitutes a surrogate figure and places the blame there. This substitution later occasions the final irony and pathos of the story.

> Of course I knew it was funny all the time. But my old man saying that right out like that sure took the kick all out of it for me and I didn't get the real kick back again ever, even when they posted the numbers upon the board and the bell rang to pay off and we saw that Kircubbin paid 67.50 for 10. All round people were saying, 'Poor Kzar! Poor Kzar!' And I

thought, I wish I were a jockey and could have rode him instead of that son of a bitch. And that was funny, thinking of George Gardner as a son of a bitch because I'd always liked him and besides he'd given us the winner, but I guess that's what he is, all right. (200)

When Joe condemns the jockey for what he has done, he has at the same time unknowingly applied the same imprecation to his own father. George has not done anything that the father had not already done in Milan. Moreover, the fact that Joe can make a moral judgment at this point implies that he is already on the verge of severing himself from the father. For a brief interval in the story the boy and the father come together after this. But once the boy becomes aware of the weakness of those around him, it cannot be long before he realizes its existence in his own father.

In the final portion of the story the father dies. Ironically, he dies on his own horse trying to win a race legitimately. If the temporary restoration of the father has caused the boy to slip back into the role of innocent at the knee of the father-protector, the regression is short-lived. And the ultimate irony is that the boy is left with a surrogate father in whom he has no faith. The father substitute in this case is the same George Gardner that Joe has condemned for pulling the horse in the fixed race. Just after the accident, Joe overhears two men talking. Their description of his father forces him to focus on the pathos of a boy who has lost the illusions of boyhood:

"Well, Butler got his, all right."

The other guy said, "I don't give a good goddam if he did, the crook. He had it coming to him on the stuff he's pulled."

"I'll say he had," said the other guy, and tore the bunch of tickets in two.

And George Gardner looked at me to see if I'd heard and I had all right and he said, "Don't you listen to what those bums said, Joe. Your old man was one swell guy."

But I don't know. Seems like when they get started they don't leave a guy nothing. (205)

The recurrent appearance of the father figure at an important juncture in the life of the Hemingway hero prefigures the appearance in the later fiction of another significant personage who similarly appears at important intervals in the protagonist's life. This figure has been called the "code hero."[1] On one level of interpretation he illustrates the "code" by which a man might live in an unpredictable universe where a contingent fate seems to have planted a snare at every quarter. This personage usually appears as a knowing old man — Count Greffi in *A Farewell to Arms* and Anselmo in *For Whom the Bell Tolls* are outstanding examples — and always he plays a key role in a fateful or climactic decision by the protagonist. His appearance in the later fiction, as the hero grows progressively older, is not accidental but a conscious part of Hemingway's treatment of the theme of self-discovery. As the wise old man or helper figure he is a reflection of one of the major archetypal figures to be found in classic and mythic lore, and Hemingway utilizes the device to further his examination of the hero's development.

Chapter IV

Threshold Experiences

"THE KILLERS" ADEQUATELY SERVES as a transition story in Hemingway's development of the central character of his stories from adolescence into young manhood. The psychological implications of that state are reflected by symbolic allusion and are equated with an introduction into evil. In many ways this story takes as a referent the biblical story of the fall of Adam, for it relates in a similar fashion the implications of acquiring a knowledge of good and evil.

In "The Snows of Kilimanjaro," when Harry, the protagonist, is very close to dying with a gangrenous leg, he tells his wife about death: " 'Never believe any of that about a scythe and a skull,' he told her, 'It can be two bicycle policemen as easily, or be a bird. Or it can have a wide snout like a hyena' " (74). In "The Killers," death comes to Nick in the form of two almost comic gangster caricatures dressed in tight black overcoats, derby hats, and black gloves. When the two speak, they do so in a stereotyped gangland jargon: " 'You're a pretty bright boy, aren't you?' " The irony of Nick's introduction to evil in this guise is that this particular serio-comic mani-

63

festation of evil is what prompts him to leave the secure confines of the small town.

When evil enters the protected world of the innocent, it cannot be escaped by a simple refusal to remain at the particular point of penetration. Once the sure knowledge of its existence has been gained, flight may be possible, but the loss of innocence can never be denied. The logical extension of this lesson forms the basis for the irony upon which the thematic contents of the "The Killers" hinge. After the killers have invaded Summit, Nick's desire "to get out of this town" in order to avoid the certain knowledge of Ole Andreson's death is ludicrous. He cannot, in fact, ever escape the implications of his experience. The choice of flight merely reflects his unwillingness to face the consequences of his knowledge. Ironically, for Nick as the character who appears in subsequent stories, the course to which he commits himself here is one which will later project him onward into further experience.

There are many signs of Nick's coming break from the local and protective ground. Several details point to the notion that something is all wrong in Nick's world. The place where the initial action occurs is known as "Henry's Lunch-Room," but it belongs to a man named George; it is not really a lunch-room but a converted barroom; the clock on the wall runs twenty minutes fast, a fact which has some importance since the killers expect Andreson at six o'clock. In the rooming house Nick mistakes a woman named Mrs. Bell for Mrs. Hirsch, the owner. Since the length of the story is about three thousand words, these details take on a sharpened focus that cannot be overlooked. Nor does Hemingway intend them to be, for they serve as a suggestive background of details which are symbolic of a world "out of joint." Hemingway uses this conventional device to heighten suspense and foreshadow the coming events which force Nick to finally leave the familiar ground and begin a journey toward selfhood.

T. S. Eliot has illustrated the same sort of conditions in *The Waste Land*.

> Here one can neither stand nor lie nor sit
> There is not even silence in the mountains
> But dry sterile thunder without rain
> There is not even solitude in the mountains
> But red sullen faces sneer and snarl
> From mudcracked houses.[1]

One would not want to make too much of the wasteland theme here; yet Hemingway depicts a boy on the threshold of adulthood, and the patterns of motifs within the psychology of such an individual are identical with those of mythological lore. In a situation which parallels the wasteland, the boy as a true hero must perform a heroic task, and this must spring from a moral impulse. When Nick cannot stand the thought of the fate of Andreson, this impulse is brought into play. If his decision to leave the town is prompted by a youthful repulsion at the thought of death, a positive impetus activates him just as much as the childish desire to escape. The hero himself must be willing to meet the trial of overcoming the powerful forces which isolate him from contact with the real world. Nick does respond at one level, but the irony lies in the fact that his flight away from himself is really one toward discovery of himself.

This course of an individual response, like all attempts to achieve individuation, is long, dangerous, and tedious, and the hero has many levels of development through which he must pass. Hemingway depicts only the articulation of the desire to separate from the involvements of the protected sphere. What any hero must do, however, is to relate and reconcile external phenomena to his own inner plight. In this respect, as Joseph Campbell has said, the first work of the hero is to "retreat from the world scene of secondary effects to those causal zones of the psyche where the difficulties really reside, and there to clarify the difficulties, eradicate them in his own case . . . and break through to the undistorted, direct experience and assimilate what C. G. Jung has called the archetypal images."[2]

This account of the psychological reverberations in an individual may seem too far from the point at hand, but its relevancy may be more clearly seen when the story is viewed as an extension of the motif of the nursery drama. Here, just as in the biblical account of the Fall, all the central symbols of the archetypal construct are employed. Like the child who must overcome certain forces which would contain him or restrict his development, the adolescent faces restrictive factors in his attempt to reach the next stage of the maturation process. That the story is an extension of the nursery drama is evident from the roles assigned to the main characters. There is here the same ineffectual father-hero figure of the boyhood stories — Ole Andreson; there is the same "nay-saying" romantic refusal to become involved in the situation, typical of the mother figure — the negro cook; and there is the arbiter guide figure — George, the owner of the lunch-room. When the two killers enter the scene and force certain reactions and responses from these characters, an obvious symbolic interlude is activated.

After the two killers have left the lunch-room, the characters directly reveal their functions. Significantly, the cook, who performs the female function of feeding, responds first: " 'I don't want any more of that.' " Nick, on the other hand, not yet fully aware of the ramifications of the experience takes the adolescent pose: "Nick stood up. He had never had a towel in his mouth before. 'Say,' he said. 'What the hell.' He was trying to swagger it off." At this point Nick still sees a certain amount of movie-thriller romance in having been tied up by movie-like gangsters. Hemingway has prepared for this by having one of the killers tell George earlier: " 'You ought to go to the movies more. The movies are fine for a bright boy like you.' " At this point, however, since it all seems to turn out all right, Nick reflects an attitude which indicates he feels the incident has no further import than the immediate situational discomfort. But George gives Nick an insight into the full implication of the visit of the killers: " 'They were going to kill Ole Andreson,' George said. 'They were going to shoot him when he came in to eat' " (286).

When Nick decides to warn Andreson, at George's suggestion, we again see the cook functioning as the wooing mother-surrogate who would keep the child from acquiring the knowledge of the world that will force the separation from the protective fold.

"You better not have anything to do with it at all," Sam, the cook, said. "You better stay way out of it."

"Don't go if you don't want to," George said.

"Mixing up in this ain't going to get you anywhere," the cook said. "You stay out of it."

"I'll go see him," Nick said to George. "Where does he live?"

The cook turned away.

"Little boys always know what they want to do," he said.

"He lives up at Hirsch's rooming-house," George said to Nick.

"I'll go up there." (286)

Nick denies the efficacy of the advice which would protect him and keep him from the impending hurt. The guide he follows is George, who in a matter-of-fact fashion pushes Nick on into the further experience. This experience will give him insight into the far-reaching effects of the presence of the seemingly "comic" killers.

Apparently Nick images the figure of Ole Andreson as having all the accouterments of the athlete-hero. As such, Andreson reflects in this role the attributes of the traditional culture hero who summarizes the aims and attitudes of the whole culture. In this way he further symbolizes all authority figures or leaders, and his actions are representative of the tendencies of all members of that culture. But something is wrong with Andreson: "'I guess he don't feel well,'" Mrs. Bell tells Nick. Lying in his bed awaiting his fate and apparently incapable of any positive action to avoid it, Andreson exhibits the qualities of the traditional wounded hero-king. The adolescent Nick hurrying to the chamber of the sick hero is a perfect parallel to the hero in the traditional Grail stories.

The possibility of restoring the "King," Ole Andreson, in this instance is an illusion. Hemingway portrays this in a sequence of exchanges, which also point to Nick's still adolescent naïveté. Nick believes that one can do something about his plight, and he cannot readily accept Andreson's refusal to act. When Andreson says, "'There isn't anything I can do about it,'" Nick cannot believe him. "'I'll tell you what they were like,'" Nick urges. But Andreson doesn't care, and Nick tries to suggest remedies for a situation that for Andreson in his state of mind has no remedy.

"Don't you want me to go and see the police?"

"No," Ole Andreson said. "That wouldn't do any good."

"Isn't there something I could do?"

"No. There ain't anything to do."

"Maybe it was just a bluff."

"No. It ain't just a bluff."

. . . .

"Couldn't you get out of town?"

"No," Ole Andreson said. "I'm through with all that running around."

He looked at the wall.

"There ain't anything to do now."

"Couldn't you fix it up some way?"

"No. I got in wrong." He talked in the same flat voice. "There ain't anything to do. After a while I'll make up my mind to go out." (287-88)

The exchange between Nick and Ole Andreson serves to illustrate dialectically the education of Nick Adams the adolescent. As the old, "wounded" hero, Ole Andreson catalogues for Nick the precise shortcomings of all possibilities of action. Flight, police authority, "fixing," all are possibilities tried and tested and proved ineffectual by the old hero in past experiences. He is the experienced one who has taken the journey in the past and knows the answers. As such, he is the *imago* of the father and at the same time the portrait of what the young hero himself might become.

Ironically, Nick's final response to the whole affair, " 'I'm going to get out of this town,' " is the reflex of what Andreson has revealed to him in the previous dialectic of learning. The Swede, having tried or considered all methods of escape from the inevitable, accepts his fate and will soon "make up his mind" to go out. He is the "sick" hero fixated at a level of inaction. This attitude of Andreson's reveals him as a hero who has failed because of some personal inadequacy. The still young Nick elects flight because to experience vicariously the same fate as that of the Swede is "too damned awful" for him at his level of development. Thus he illustrates his refusal to accept the inadequacies typified by the Swede. He is not able to accept the matter-of-fact adjustment represented by George, either, and he must elect another way. The course he does choose is the seemingly protective one of the dark, hermaphroditic mother-guide figure of the cook who won't "even listen to it." But the collective forces of experience will not leave Nick unscarred. If he thinks to elude the inevitable by leaving, Hemingway leaves no doubt that he cannot. Just as the killers have come into this sphere from that beyond, so Nick will encounter identical forces in his flight.

Hemingway explores the plight of a Nick Adams who has made the decision reached in "The Killers" in two other short stories, "The Battler" and "The Light of the World." Both of these stories depict a character who has left the town of his upbringing and is in flight from the experiences of his youth. And both of the stories are significant in the whole of Hemingway's treatment of the learning experience of his central character. If the young hero has had his sensibility scarred by the experiences of youth in the protective environment of home, then these two episodes in his flight are demonstrative of a further and more serious introduction into the machinations of the world. Here is revealed a world of nightmarish experience where things are amiss, and both stories illustrate to some extent a desire to recover a world where the comfort and security of the lost home and mother are established.

In "The Battler," Hemingway revolves the plot around the motif of "the promise given and the promise withdrawn." This device forcefully points up Nick's alienation from the protective sphere which implies, romantically, that all promises given will be fulfilled. Further, the operation of the motif is intensified by the contrasting light and dark symbols which form the opposite poles of attraction and repulsion in the middle-ground on which the hero finds himself.

Nick's first introduction into a world where promises are not kept forms the early coincidence of his involvement in the central drama by the fireside

of a punchdrunk ex-fighter and an apparently homosexual Negro. In the opening scene, having just been
thrown from a train, Nick stands near the railroad
tracks with his trousers torn, his knees skinned, and
his hands scraped.

> That lousy crut of a brakeman. He would get
> him some day. He would know him again.
> That was a fine way to act.
>   "Come here, kid," he said. "I got something for
> you."
>   He had fallen for it. What a lousy kid thing
> to have done. They would never suck him in
> that way again.
>   "Come here, kid, I got something for you."
> Then *wham* and he lit on his hands and knees
> beside the track. (129)

This first instance serves to reveal Nick's discovery
that a simple, childlike response will not serve in relationships with individuals outside of the protected
family circle. Also, the brakeman is one of a long list
of authority figures who does not fulfill the expected
role for the innocent. Even the language Hemingway
uses here is suggestive of the infantile relationship:
" 'Come here, kid, I got something for you,' " echoes
some sort of offer of candy or some other desirable
object that a child might expect to be given by an
adult. The result has an effect far more significant
than Nick's being thrown from a train, for the brakeman's action cuts to the quick of Nick's childish response. What Nick feels here is shame and mortifica-
tion at having been lured by the authority figure into
playing the role of the child. Nick's vow that "they"
shall never do it to him again illustrates his adolescent

anger rather than a true learning experience, however, for in the very next scene he again becomes the victim of the same kind of lure.

The second instance of the promise given and the ready acceptance of such a promise from another authority figure precipitates a more profound learning situation for Nick. Walking along the tracks Nick sees a fire off in the darkness. Hemingway invokes certain traditional symbols at this point, for Nick is walking easily and solidly along the tracks, suggestive of the motif of "The Way." In mythology, as in *Pilgrim's Progress*, this signifies the tried and proved path. As long as the hero adheres to it he is protected by benevolent forces. Alongside the tracks there is a swamp, another traditional image. In mythic terms it is representative of the labyrinthian passages of the unconscious and irrational. Whenever the hero is lured from the tried and proved pathway the dangers symbolized by the swamp threaten to swallow him and to terminate his journey into self-discovery. The same sort of symbolic interplay operates here, for when Nick, hungry and tired, sees the firelight just off the tracks in the swamp the temptation is too great: "He must get to somewhere." Yet Nick is only a few miles from a town, Mancelona, and if he continues along the true pathway he will soon be out of the swamp. Just as Christian in his journey strayed many times from the path, however, so Nick does here and the consequences are not greatly different from those related in *Pilgrim's Progress*.

With the lesson impressed upon him so recently by the brakeman, Nick approaches the fire carefully. He soon drops his guard — a childish regression —

and in this way the lesson not totally learned from
the train experience is more subtly taught him again.
At the fire Nick finds the degenerate, ex-prizefighter
Ad Francis, who offers him hospitality and food. The
initial exchange between the two is indicative of a
kind of adjustment to the world which refers back to
Nick's earlier response to the brakeman.

> "It must have made him feel good to bust
> you," the man said seriously.
> "I'll bust him."
> "Get him with a rock sometime when he's
> going through," the man advised.
> "I'll get him."
> "You're a tough one, aren't you?"
> "No," Nick answered.
> "All you kids are tough."
> "You got to be tough," Nick said.
> "That's what I said." (131)

As in "The Killers," Hemingway employs a short
dialectical discourse between an authority-hero figure
and the young Nick to illustrate a possible adjustment
to the circumstances of the world. The credo of adjustment postulated by Francis and repeated by Nick
— tough, tough, tough — is often thought to be the
dominant attitude held by all Hemingway heroes in
all situations. This story amply illustrates that it is
not, for Hemingway interjects a foreign element which
forces a reconsideration on Nick's part of Francis'
answer to the problems of the world.

With the preparation of the food by Bugs,
Francis, who has already asked Nick if he was hungry,

begins to "change" — a signal of his chronic illness. He soon becomes irrational and challenges Nick.

> "You're a hot sketch. Who the hell asked you to butt in here?"
> "Nobody."
> "You're damn right nobody did. Nobody asked you to stay either. You come in here and act snotty about my face and smoke my cigars and drink my liquor and then talk snotty. Where the hell do you think you get off?"
> Nick said nothing. Ad stood up.
> "I'll tell you, you yellow-livered Chicago bastard. You're going to get your can knocked off. Do you get that?" (135)

The withdrawal of the promise and the threat of personal violence points to an important learning experience for Nick. As the athlete-hero, Francis functions in somewhat the same manner as Andreson in "The Killers": his "sickness" adumbrates the cultural plight of a whole civilization into which Nick is being thrust. The features of Francis directly portray the inner state of degeneracy: "In the firelight Nick saw that his face was misshapen. His nose was sunken, his eyes were slits, he had queer-shaped lips. Nick did not perceive all this at once, he only saw the man's face was queerly formed and mutilated. It was like putty in color. Dead looking in the firelight." And what is more, Francis has only one ear, a fact which makes Nick "a little sick" (131). The distortion of the fighter's features prefigure exactly what Nick learns about him and is a distant extension of what

Nick learned about the Swede. Francis is "sick," and his sickness is both physical and moral.

Nick's nausea over the disfigurement of the fighter and his subsequent insight into the moral plight of this hero figure is similar to the reaction of many of the central characters of the stories. Sometimes they can articulate what they feel about the sordid moral state of the sick or pseudo hero, and usually they feel as the narrator of "The Mother of a Queen" does toward a homosexual bullfighter. He asks, "What kind of blood is it that makes a man like that?" (419). At his stage of development Nick can only feel a sense of uncertainty and repulsion. But the insight the encounter with Bugs and Francis provides at least paves the way for a later, conscious awareness of evil.

In a symbolic frame of reference, as the sick hero Francis is also the ogre figure with whom Nick must do battle on the threshold of maturity. In this sense he is symbolic of the father-authority who is both the helpful guide and the dangerous presence guarding the entrance into the unknown. The fighter here stands as the father who has held out the promise to the hero as a child but who withdrew the promise. The ironic function of the fighter is more clearly seen in this instance when the details of setting are taken into account. The whole of the drama takes place around a fire, a conventional symbol of light and hope; here, however, the events that take place are suggestive of violence and evil, and the traditional usage is inverted. When Nick comes out of the night just "wounded" from his ordeal with the brakeman, he is duped into expecting comfort and sustenance by the campfire. But that promise is withdrawn, and he is forced to continue on his journey.

At the fireside Bugs gives Nick an extra sandwich to help him along the way, and here a further irony is revealed. Functioning in much the same fashion as the cook in "The Killers," the Negro here is the cook and soother, the hermaphroditic figure who resembles the mother. He controls the situation at all times, in spite of his deferential treatment of both Francis and Nick. The fact that he is dark, however, signals the danger inherent in the nature of such a figure. His apparent homosexuality gives further credence to his changeling nature and points to the dangers of the personage who indulges in activities which are *contra naturam*. Steeped in ambiguity, this figure reveals a dangerous nature — he "changes" Francis by tapping him at the base of the skull with a blackjack; and a protective one — he tells Nick to leave, giving him directions and food.

In this dual role the Negro is typical of the traditional herald figure drawn in sharp outline form, and he conforms to Joseph Campbell's description: "The herald or announcer of the adventure, therefore, is often dark, loathly, or terrifying, judged evil by the world; yet if one could follow, the way would be opened through the walls of day into the dark where the jewels glow. Or the herald is a beast (as in the fairy tale), representative of the repressed instinctual fecundity within ourselves, or again a veiled mysterious figure — the unknown."[3] It is Bugs who saves Nick from the encounter with Francis and prevents him from remaining at this lesser level of development. Defeat by the authority-father figure would mean that the hero has not yet reached the point of development required for the journey he has already undertaken. Bugs steps in at this point as the helper figure, and the catastrophic results of a defeat are avoided.

Involved in this symbolic interlude by the fireside are other associative connotations which reinforce the thematic implications of the "promise withdrawn" motif. The disfigured hero represented by Francis is part of a whole series of wounded or crippled heroes that appear in Hemingway's fiction. Philip Young has pointed out the significance of the wound for Nick Adams in a discussion of the "Chapter VI" sketch of *In Our Time:* "This culminating blow in the spine is symbol and climax for a process that has been going on since we first met Nick; it is an outward and visible sign of an inward and spiritual dis-grace."[4] Also, William Bysshe Stein has observed: "The Freudian roll call of symbolic phallic wounds in [Hemingway's] works is interminable. Nick is injured in the leg and Robert Jordan in the thigh. Harry in 'The Snows of Kilimanjaro' dies of a gangrened limb; Colonel Cantwell wears a scar on his knee; Harry Morgan in *To Have and Have Not* loses an arm; Lieutenant Henry in *A Farewell To Arms* and Jake Barnes in *The Sun Also Rises* are comparably afflicted."[5] But along with signifying an outward token of an inner attitude and of being suggestive of emotional hurts, the symbolic wound is a cipher which takes as its key the manifold, cognate myths of crippled heroes. Only by apprehending this function can the frequent occurrences of the wound be seen as an integral part of a basic, recurring theme.

The significance of the wounded hero takes on dimension when viewed in the light of the broader motif of the crippled hero. Jacob, Christ, Paul, Oedipus, and Samson, to mention only a few obvious examples from biblical and classical sources, all are part of a series of redemptive heroes who were crippled or abandoned in some fashion in their particular struggles with contingent forces. The motif has been described by James Clark Moloney, and he indicates some of the main configurations of its workings.

The crippled, rejected hero is a unique concept. The vicissitudes of the hero's life have been sung in the sagas of almost every culture. There is an attention-riveting quality about this hero. No matter from whence he came, this ubiquitous male was stereotyped. Almost always his birth has been predicted. The hero was born to save mankind. Frequently he was the son of a virgin. If not the son of a virgin, then the hero's father was a god. Rather universally a jealous person in power — an uncle, father or grandfather — attempted to kill the hero. To escape this menace the hero was separated from his family. He was reared by strangers in a strange land. These heroes were crippled as well as abandoned. Finally, the hero's day of destiny arrives. The hero returns and kills the brutal ruler, or the hero after an upsurge of activity is himself killed. The hero's death is often a scapegoat death, serving the utilitarian purpose of perpetuating life (Leviticus, Chapter 16, Verses 5-10). After he is dead, the hero returns to the earth that often rejuvenates him, effectuates his rebirth or resurrection.[6]

What these parallels serve to illustrate is that Hemingway's plan to depict a redemptive hero grounds itself primarily upon a universal pattern of motifs. When these stories are viewed from this perspective, not so obvious undertones appear.

What Nick sees that makes him "a little sick" is literally that Francis has only one ear, but what he has experienced by the end of "The Battler" leaves him somewhat confused. The experience teaches him that the answer he thought he had at the beginning — be tough — is not valid in all situations. His final view of the ex-prizefighter directly contradicts what he had been led to expect from the athlete-hero. If Francis bears the signs of the redemptive hero, he more pointedly personifies the unredeemed hero. Francis is caught in the swamp of a labyrinthian night-world from which there is no possible escape. In this respect, he is much like the Swede in "The Killers." The dark conductor, Bugs, has led him into the swamp. But as in all heroic cycles the conductor is not at fault for the hero's plight. As Bugs tells Nick, Francis has not only taken too many beatings but was involved in an "incestuous" affair, squandered all his money, and took to "busting people all the time." His alienation from all social intercourse is a logical extension of his inner difficulties. He is held prisoner, therefore, by the shadow figure of Bugs, who by further extension is representative of the repressed and irrational side of Francis' own self. The guilt of his incest and all the scarring experiences — beatings — he has suffered are what really hold this hero in bondage. Nick, as the hero-becoming and the young man on the journey toward self-learning, is presented with a perfect example of the hero who has failed in the quest.

Hemingway's purpose in these short stories is not to relate the final outcome of the learning experiences Nick undergoes. More important is the dramatization of the experiences themselves and the revelation of the impact they have upon the central character. By the end of this story the obvious point is made that the title refers to the young Nick and his active engagement in the struggle of life, not to Francis, except ironically. "The Battler" relates to the process of maturation Nick is undergoing, and the particular trial depicted in the story is only one of the many that he will encounter throughout life.

Nick's further exposure in another story, "The Light of the World," is depicted in a highly ironic fashion. As in "The Killers," Hemingway employs an assortment of serio-comic characters, and here he invokes a burlesque interlude in order to explore the deadly serious implications of an encounter with evil. The title is excerpted from the New Testament story of Christ's encounter with the woman taken in adultery.[7] When Christ disposes of the arguments of the scribes and Pharisees He remarks: "I am the light of the world: he that followeth me shall not walk in darkness, but shall have the light of life" (John 8:12). Viewed in this context the title has a multiple significance in relation to the major thematic emphasis of the story.

The situation depicted is one in which Nick is again at large in the world. Nick is accompanied by a friend, Tom, who serves as a register against which Nick's responses may be tested. Both are young men

who have just arrived in a strange town. The place is
unusual, and their first encounter with a townsman, a
bartender, is answered with hostility. Here, too, as
in "The Killers," there is something amiss. Tom senses
this and remarks at one point, " 'What the hell kind
of place is this?' " (385). After their encounter with
the barman, they go to the train station where they
meet an unlikely aggregation: "Down at the station
there were five whores waiting for the train to come in,
and six white men and four Indians" (385). Again,
there is something wrong. Nick, the narrator of this
piece, suggests: "It was crowded and hot from the
stove and full of stale smoke. As we came in nobody
was talking and the ticket window was down" (385).
With the entry of Nick and Tom the atmosphere
changes somewhat. What follows is a curious parody
of the traditional "affirmation of the faith," in which
two of the prostitutes describe their more than close
relationship with the fighter, Stanley Ketchel.

The exposure is to an abnormal situation which
has the aura of the normal, and there are two major
movements in the story which serve to focus upon the
impact of this experience. The details of setting and
the responses of the barman in the first portion of
the narrative prefigure the underlying implications not
readily apparent in the second. Tom seems the more
experienced of the two boys, and in the exchange that
takes place in the barroom he is the active participant.
The bartender decides to serve them only after he has
seen that they have money, and Tom, who earlier
had been stopped by the bartender from eating the
free-lunch pig's feet, responds angrily to the bartender's hostility and suspicion. Nick, on the other

hand, acts in a more level-headed manner and tries to soothe the situation.

> "Your goddam pig's feet stink," Tom said, and spit what he had in his mouth on the floor. The bartender didn't say anything. The man who had drunk the rye paid and went out without looking back.
>
> "You stink yourself," the bartender said. "All you punks stink."
>
> "He says we're punks," Tommy said to me.
>
> "Listen," I said. "Let's get out."
>
> "You punks clear the hell out of here," the bartender said.
>
> "I said we were going out," I said. "It wasn't your idea."
>
> "We'll be back," Tommy said.
>
> "No you won't," the bartender told him.
>
> "Tell him how wrong he is," Tom turned to me.
>
> "Come on," I said. (385)

In the second portion of the story Nick begins to participate in the action more aggressively, and in the conclusion the point of the story is illustrated by the degree of his involvement.

> Alice looked at her and then at us and her face lost that hurt look and she smiled and she had about the prettiest face I ever saw. She had a pretty face and a nice smooth skin and a lovely voice and she was nice all right and really friendly. But my God she was big. She was as big as three women. Tom saw me looking at her and he said, "Come on. Let's go."

"Good-bye," said Alice. She certainly had a nice voice. "Good-bye," I said. (390-91)

Nick has earlier told one of the men in the station, a homosexual cook, that his and Tom's ages are "seventeen and nineteen." Since he is the speaker, it may be assumed that the first figure refers to himself. This is of importance to the characterization in the story, for here Tom, as the older more experienced one, urges Nick away from the hint of temptation suggested by Nick's "looking" at Alice. The initial situation with the barman is reversed, for now Tom withdraws. An examination of the underlying symbolic drama which formulates the dynamic configuration of this story illustrates the meaning of the reversal of roles.

The whole of the central force of the interlude at the train station takes as its motif the burlesque elevation of Stanley Ketchel, a prizefighter, into the role of an imitation Christ. Once again, as in "The Killers" and "The Battler," Nick is given the measure of a counterfeit hero in the role of the perennial, redemptive hero. But what is not immediately evident is that he is being told the tale of such a personage, for Hemingway has so devised the situation that the absurd attitudes of the prostitutes seem at one level to have validity.

The repetition throughout of allusions and direct references to deity charges the burlesque situation to such a point that the whole scene is transformed into a kind of absurd Walpurgis Night. Nick as the young would-be initiate views the attestation of faith and renewal of vows of two prostitutes to the arch-god of physicality represented by Ketchel. Their physical proportions and subsequent conversation suggest that they are embodiments of the Seven Deadly Sins: pride, covetousness, lust, anger, gluttony, envy, and sloth. The mediator-priest present here is the homosexual cook — "his face was white and his hands were white and thin," and he plays his role throughout: " 'Can't you stop that sort of thing?' the cook asked. 'Can't we speak decently?' " (388).

Ironically enough, in a complete reversal of the conventional usage of black and white imagery, the mock "white-Christ" has been defeated by a Negro. One of the prostitutes recounts the story of the defeat, and her telling enforces the burlesque character of the interlude.

> "It was a trick," Peroxide said. "That big dinge took him by surprise. He'd just knocked Jack Johnson down, the big black bastard. That nigger beat him by a fluke."
>
> The ticket window went up and the three Indians went over to it.
>
> "Steve knocked him down," Peroxide said, "He turned to smile at me."
>
> "I thought you said you weren't on the coast," some one said.
>
> "I went out just for that fight. Steve turned to smile at me and that black son of a bitch from hell jumped up and hit him by surprise. Steve could lick a hundred like that black bastard." (389)

The ironic reversal of the conventional "white equals good, black equals bad" formula adds verisimilitude to the apparent seriousness of the character in her description of the fight. For her, Ketchel represents the forces of "good," and his defeat by Johnson is indicative of the operation of Satanic forces. The whole incident as she describes it is a direct parallel with Christ's struggle with Satan in the desert, only in this account the pseudo-Christ is defeated.

Another detail which Hemingway imposes to add further to the parallel occurs in a reference made by one of the prostitutes: " 'Steve Ketchel,' one of the blondes said in a high voice as though the name had pulled a trigger in her. 'His own father shot and killed him. Yes, by Christ, his own father. There aren't any more men like Steve Ketchel' " (388). The reference here suggests the Crucifixion and Christ's appeal to God, His father. Other references throughout further substantiate the device Hemingway has employed: " 'He was like a god, he was' " (389), and " 'He was the greatest, finest, whitest, most beautiful man that ever lived, Steve Ketchel, and his own father shot him down like a dog' " (388).

That these are the "brides" of the mock-Christ figure is illustrated by their "affirmation of the faith" and by their grotesque revelations of the degree that each was the "true" bride. Their remarks directly echo the traditional taking of the vows by nuns who become the "bride of Christ." In the argument, for example, one of the prostitutes illustrates this: " 'He was more than any husband could ever be.' Peroxide said. 'We were married in the eyes of God and I belong to him right now and always will and all of me is his. I don't care about my body. They can take my body. My soul belongs to Steve Ketchel' " (389). In response the other prostitute relates her experience: "Alice was crying so she could hardly speak from shaking so. 'He said, "You're a lovely piece, Alice." That's exactly what he said' " (390). The culmination of the argument sequence occurs with Alice besting the other prostitute by a ludicrous appraisal of her value, both in relation to Ketchel and to the present: " 'No,' Alice said in that sweet lovely voice, 'you haven't got any real memories except having your tubes out and when you started C. and M. Everything else you just read in the papers. I'm clean and you know it and men like me, even though I'm big, and you know it, and I never lie and you know it' " (390).

Nick and Tom have been listening to the exchange, but the younger Nick is taken in by the seductive voice and appearance of the "Queen," who emerges victorious in this Walpurgis Night congregation. Nick describes the features of Alice as almost Madonnalike: "She had a pretty face and a nice smooth skin and a lovely voice." But it is the older Tom ("I swear to Christ I've never been anywhere like this" [387].) who guides Nick away from the dangers of involvement with the apparently real diabolic forces at work. When the cook asks, " 'Which way are you boys going?' " his question is one laden with meaning in the light of the experience Nick and Tom have just encountered. In his sympathetic attitude toward Alice, Nick might be ready to choose the "wrong" way. Tom, however, is the forceful agent who literally saves Nick from himself and the possibility of being imprisoned in this "Palace of Lucifera." " 'The other way from you' " (391), Tom tells the cook, and his words also have a prophetic cast to them in relation to the symbolic frame of the experience with these representa-

f the Seven Deadly Sins. Nick does not make a
ous moral choice here, but his "guide" represents in a psychological framework another aspect of
his own personality. If the "guide" leads him away
from the dangers represented, it is some indication
that he has escaped the dangers of the irrational at
one point. He will be able to cope better with similar
circumstances in the normal, everyday world where
identical forces are encountered in more subtle guises.

Hemingway's intense interest in the threshold
encounters with the dark forces of the world by a
young hero are not limited solely to the Nick Adams
stories. In "The Revolutionist" and in "The Capital
of the World," he deals with similar encounters. Both
of these stories suggest opposing responses by the
two young heroes who are the central characters of
each. The narrative method differs in both, and the
themes account for the difference in approach. In
"The Revolutionist," the narrator relates the adventure of a young man with romantic illusions who
keeps them, although it is obvious that is all they are.
In "The Capital of the World," the direct threshold
experience is revealed, and although the central character also has romantic illusions about life there is
illustrated here the account of the vital moment of
facing reality.

No more than a brief sketch, the significance
of "The Revolutionist" is more in its focus upon the
young central character than as a short story with
all the traditional accouterments of that form. In
the opening lines, the narrator, a worker for the
"movement" in Italy, describes the credentials the
young man carries: "In 1919 he was travelling on

the railroads in Italy, carrying a square of oilcloth from the headquarters of the party written in indelible pencil and saying here was a comrade who had suffered very much under the Whites in Budapest and requesting comrades to aid him in any way. He used this instead of a ticket. He was very shy and quite young and the train men passed him on from one crew to another. He had no money, and they fed him behind the counter in railway eating houses" (157).

The irony implied by the title of the piece becomes apparent, for this is a "revolutionist" traveling with "false" credentials. Having experienced war and "suffered much" he has no conception of the implications of that suffering, and his attitudes belie the literal message of his credentials. He is still the innocent untouched by experience, much as the young Nick in "Indian Camp." Here, however, the young revolutionary is not a boy of Nick's age; he is a young man who has experienced the wider, more expansive happenings in the socio-political realm. This is an area of experience into which Hemingway thrusts other young heroes as they progressively grow older. Having gone through the period of childhood and young adolescence, there are certain kinds of responses to be expected of the young adult. If he maintains his childish illusions through his young manhood, the initial awakening experience will have traumatic consequences. Played against the register of the older and more experienced narrator, the young hero depicts an individual who is still fixed at some infantile level.

The naïve innocence of the young revolutionist

and his inability to see the far-reaching consequences of the acts in which he is involved are brought into focus by the single exchange cited between him and the narrator of this sketch.

> He was a Magyar, a very nice boy and very shy. Horthy's men had done some bad things to him. He talked about it a little. In spite of Hungary, he believed altogether in the world revolution.
>
> "But how is the movement going in Italy?" he asked.
>
> "Very badly," I said.
>
> "But it will go better," he said. "You have everything here. It is the one country that every one is sure of. It will be the starting point of everything."
>
> I did not say anything. (157)

The juxtaposition of the narrator's pessimism and the young man's optimism points up the themes of illusion and disillusion that appear throughout Hemingway's short stories. In this story the themes are related to a cause as an ideal. In the stories that refer to an older character, Hemingway sometimes parallels such attachments to the cleavage of the infant to its mother. Both kinds of attachments have dangers, and the maturation process which must follow involves a separation from dependency, insight into the nature of all protective agencies, and final atonement as the self emerges. In the exchange between the narrator and the young boy, author sympathy seems to lie with the older of the pair. Be that as it may, there is still a certain nostalgia indicated in the narrator's attitude toward the boy with ideals. Thus this story is not so much an indictment of the ideal as it is an examination of the individuals who are romantically committed to it.

The boy is on his way to Switzerland, and for him it represents refuge and freedom from the trials of the movement. The boy wishes to walk over the pass from Italy into Switzerland, a further indication in this context of his romantic propensities. As the narrator tells of his final association with the boy and of his knowledge of the boy's fate, a final, subtle irony emerges: "He thanked me very much, but his mind was already looking forward to walking over the pass. He was very eager to walk over the pass while the weather held good. He loved the mountains in the autumn. The last I heard of him the Swiss had him in jail near Sion" (158). The reference to the boy's imprisonment implies the restriction of reality being imposed upon the free, naïve spirit of the boy's idealism. The insinuation is of such a slight degree that it serves only to prefigure coming possibilities. The boy will learn what the narrator already knows but about which he cannot "say anything" in the face of the boy's impassioned idealism.

Life on the threshold of maturation does not always end with only a slight hint of what is to come, however, and Hemingway depicts the pathos and supreme danger of the experience in another story, "The Capital of the World." Here, a young boy fresh from the provinces has come to Madrid to work as a waiter. His great fantasy is that he could become a brave bullfighter if only he had the chance. In an extremely ironical ending the boy is killed while playing at bullfighting. This occurs by accident, for he is stabbed with a knife attached to a chair and held as a "bull" by another young character, a dishwasher. This latter character plays the role of the "knowing one," for he has trained as a bullfighter but has experienced the dangers and cannot reconcile himself to them. " 'Look at that,' he said. 'And I wash dishes,' " he tells the boy, Paco, after showing him some passes with an apron. When Paco questions him about the bull ring, the dishwasher tells of his plight: " 'Fear,' said Enrique. '*Miedo*. The same fear you would have in a ring with a bull' " (46). Paco still has illusions about bravery, and so they go on to play at bullfighting with the knives.

In much the same manner as he did in "The Killers" and "The Battler," Hemingway examines the adjustments made by pseudo-cultural heroes. Here, however, the innocent, rather than being faced with the experiences of these figures directly, operates on the periphery and is exposed to contingent forces seemingly unrelated to the situational exigencies of the life that surrounds him. Yet Hemingway has so fashioned this story that the fate of the boy is intricately involved with the spiritual plight and pathetic orientation of a life of which he was literally never a part. The narrative pattern employed is a sequence of miniature portraits of the people who live at the hotel where Paco works as an apprentice waiter. These portraits are so interspersed that as the events which lead to Paco's death occur, the revelation of the character of these individuals, their personal plight, and their individual responses to their plight emerge simultaneously. The effect of this organization is such that it interweaves the individual thematic conflicts into a final over-all thematic focus which gathers meaning upon the death of Paco.

From the opening lines Hemingway imposes sufficient suggestive detail upon the characterization of Paco to illustrate that he is in a sense an *imitatio Christi*. As Hemingway relates in the story, "Paco" as a name is a diminutive of Francisco. The implication of this notation becomes evident in the details which are cited about Paco's life. In the tradition of the stranger god who enters the wasteland, Paco "had no father to forgive him, nor anything for the father to forgive." And, in a reference suggestive of Christ's place of nativity, Paco "came from a village in a part of Extramadura where conditions were incredibly primitive, food scarce, and comforts unknown and he had worked hard ever since he could remember" (38). In many of the myth references to the archetypal hero the fact that the father is unknown and the humble circumstances into which the heroic personage is born are reflections of his magical or divine nature. These outward signs prefigure the magical task to be performed by the hero in his life.

The hero must also have some outstanding personal quality which will fit him for the task and mark him as one who is different from those around him. Paco, in his adolescent-like naïveté, exhibits in mock fashion the Christian virtue of *charisma:* "He was fast on his feet and did his work well and he *loved* his sisters, who seemed beautiful and sophisticated; he *loved* Madrid, which was still an unbelievable place, and he *loved* his work which, done under bright lights, with clean linen, the wearing of evening clothes, and abundant food in the kitchen, seemed romantically beautiful" (38, italics added). But Hemingway uses this detail in both an ironic and in a serious sense. He equates *love* with innocence and naïveté. The boy is attracted to the elements around him simply because he is unsophisticated and is dazzled by them. Still, his name is really Francisco, Francis, and coupled with his unsophisticated cast of mind and humble origin it is possible that Hemingway is suggesting St. Francis of Assisi, another *imatatio Christi*. In the symbolic framework, Paco has the attributes of the traditional pastoral hero who exemplifies natural man. When such a personage comes to the sophisticated environment of the city, here Madrid, "The Capital of the World," he has literally involved himself with a direct exposure to the forces of evil. Such an encounter is bound to lead to an open breach and a clash of these two opposites.

The symbolism of this story suggests a situation with universal implications. Paco as the hero-becoming and future participant in the archetype of the hero becomes an *imitatio Christi*, and the values to which he is committed are similar to the doctrine of love in the New Testament. The resultant death of Paco by stabbing serves the same function as the Crucifixion. The world of Madrid, "The Capital of the World," Jerusalem, cannot accept the "light" brought by this pastoral figure, and he must be eradicated. This is the pattern of all savior heroes, and this is the pattern Hemingway employs as a symbolic correlative to the literal, albeit ironic theme.

The world will not accept true heroes for long, and when heroes die the danger to convention goes with them. In "Banal Story" Hemingway makes the same point in reference to the bullfighter Maera. There the focus points to the addiction of people to unimportant tabloid romances while a singular event is taking place: the death of a hero. The narrative relates the effects such a passing has on others: "Men and boys bought full-length colored pictures of him to remember him by, and lost the picture they had of him in their memories by looking at the lithographs. Bull-fighters were very relieved he was dead, because he did always in the bull-ring the things they could only do sometimes" (361).

Christ as an archetypal hero established His code through the process of individuation. He was not, however, the first culture hero to establish a moral order through the traditional life-death-rebirth pattern. Rather, Christ is one of a series of culture gods. Attis and Adonis, for example, suffered death and dismemberment, then were reborn, signifying a symbolic rejuvenation for all mankind. They, too, repeated the cycle over and over again, just as the Crucifixion and Redemption are celebrated over and over in the Christian tradition. Yet the cycle of Christ has some difference from these earlier myths, for His death was consciously accepted. As M. E. Harding has pointed out, the Resurrection not only implies a new cycle in a long list of cycles, it represents a victory over self and a symbolic transformation.[8]

Paco is faced with the necessity of making a conscious choice which ultimately relates to his own death. Although somewhat goaded into braving the knives of the mock-bull by Enrique, the "cynical and bitter" dishwasher, and although the motivation for his action is grounded in "illusion," Paco faces this threshold encounter and its dangerous forces with all the courage and nobility that he imagines real bull-fighters to have. (As the interspersed portraits of the bullfighters who live at the hotel illustrate, however, the real ones do not.) Furthermore, in a sense Paco dies for all mankind, as represented by the elements to which he has been exposed in Madrid. This is sug-gested by his inner attitudes. After listening to a dis-cussion of politics by two other waiters in the hotel restaurant, the central intelligence reveals Paco's thoughts: "Paco had said nothing. He did not yet under-stand politics but it always gave him a thrill to hear the tall waiter speak of the necessity for killing the priests and the Guardia Civil. The tall waiter repre-sented to him revolution and revolution also was romantic. He himself would like to be a good catholic, a revolutionary, and have a steady job like this, while, at the same time, being a good bullfighter" (42-43). In his effort to prove that he can face the "horns" with-out fear, Paco dies and preserves his illusions, his ideals. In this way he denies the role that the pseudo-heroes play and establishes himself in the role of the crucified hero who dies for a cause.

Hemingway imposes a heavy irony upon the death of Paco, however, and it is in this irony, once seen in the light of the broader motif, that the subtle, underlying thematic intent emerges. When Paco lies dying on the floor, Hemingway employs an unusual simile to evoke an ironic tone. He describes Paco as "feeling his life go out of him as dirty water empties from a bathtub when the plug is drawn" (50). Seemingly, the comparison would imply a negation on the author's part of the life of illusion which Paco has lived. But in the next passage Paco is described as starting an act of contrition which he does not finish. This detail echoes the opening description of Paco who "had no father to forgive him, nor anything for the father to forgive." That is, Paco is the unspotted one. Evil, death, and decay flourish around him in the lives of those who live in the hotel, but in the tradition of the saints who are elevated beyond worldly and mortal corruption, he transcends without ever being touched or tainted by evil.

In a further reinforcement of the heavy irony with which Paco's death is surrounded, Hemingway appends a closing commentary upon his life and the significance of his death: "The boy Paco had never known about any of this nor about what all these people would be doing on the next day and on other days to come. He had no idea how they really lived nor how they ended. He did not even realize they ended. He died, as the Spanish phrase has it, full of illusions. He had not had time in his life to lose any of them, nor even, at the end, to complete an act of contrition" (50-51). The repetition of the "act of contrition" here is the key to the underlying significance of the ironic reference to Paco's life going out of him like "dirty water." Paco, as saint, as god-hero, is a participant in the chthonic aspects of mortality in spite of the moral and spiritual qualities represented by his "illusions." He must therefore cleanse himself of the taint represented by those around him. When he forces the issue of the mock-bullfight, he symbolically engages in a direct fashion the forces of the dark side of man's life. But this is a threshold experience, and in order to be successful in all of its associative elements the experience is one from which the hero must emerge triumphant over the forces of instinctuality. As represented in the Christ story, the hero must emerge victorious over the dark aspects of his *own* nature, really, in order to achieve a transformation. Paco never achieves this all-important victory, for he escapes through death.

Taken in such a context, the death of Paco without any hint of the possibility of redemption implicit in the crucifixion of Christ is suggestive of the inability of an individual to achieve a reconciliation with the chthonic forces operating in the universe. Paco, however, is not condemned either by narrative tone or by descriptive detail. Rather, the complexes of symbolic formations in this story suggest that he is the pastoral hero with pastoral ideals who comes to the sophisticated city, another "Palace of Lucifera," and must be killed because there is no place in that city for such a figure.

Paco's ordeal on the threshold of learning reveals an amplification of the theme of individuation. Hemingway does not lament the passing of an ideal as he will in later stories, but the intricate interweaving of universal symbols achieves his artistic intent. Paco is only one of a series of heroes who commit themselves to an ideal and are forced to pay the consequences. His type of heroism represents only one way of dealing with the world. Another way is to "adjust," which may mean compromise, and many characters in the stories do. The threshold encounters depicted by Hemingway elucidate an important and natural part of the process of learning. The outcome of the exposure to experience may be tragic, as in the case of Paco, or it may pave the way for further trials, as in "The Killers." Hemingway's approach to both possible outcomes of the process of maturation adumbrates the direction of his examination of man's fate in the universe.

Chapter V

The War and After

PERHAPS NO OTHER SUBJECT has occupied so much of Hemingway's thought as that of war. It is one of the principal concerns of two of his most conspicuous successes in the novel form, *A Farewell to Arms* and *For Whom the Bell Tolls*. It also provides the background which activates the thematic conflict in *Across the River and into the Trees*. *Men at War,* edited by Hemingway, is an anthology of great war stories of past writers, together with two war sequences from Hemingway's novels and a news dispatch by him on the war in Spain, entitled "The Chauffeurs of Madrid." In the original short story collection *In Our Time,* Hemingway's second book, half of the miniatures are devoted to war. The final organization of *The First Forty-Nine Stories* includes about a half dozen stories dealing with war in some fashion or other, and Hemingway's only play to be produced, "The Fifth Column," also deals with war. Likewise much of Hemingway's journalism is about war experiences.

Most critics attribute this great concern with war to the same source as Hemingway's self-professed interest in the bullfight: death. Hemingway himself was the principal fostering agent for this notion, for in *Death in the Afternoon*, written in 1932, he described his fascination with death during his apprentice years as a writer. Carlos Baker's summation serves well to illustrate Hemingway's interest in the subject.

> The Castilian attitude towards death is evidently very close to Hemingway's own. Unlike the Galicians and the Catalans, who have very little feeling for death, the Castilians "have great common sense. . . . They know death is the unescapable reality, the one thing any man may be sure of. . . . They think a great deal about death and when they have a religion they have one which believes that life is much shorter than death." Since by going to the bullring they have a chance of seeing death "given, avoided, refused, and accepted," they pay their money and go. Such a healthy attitude toward death is one way of overcoming the usual sentimental taboos. To face the fact of death is as necessary to the writer of tragedy as a healthy facing of the other facts of life.[1]

It is not too difficult to accept the transition from a preoccupation with death in the bullring to death in war. In fact, both war and bullfighting have always been recognized as the major metaphorical bases for much of Hemingway's fiction. Since both emphasize the importance of adjustment to death, this common denominator provides a view of the interworkings of Hemingway's artistry when it concerns itself with either bullfighting or war.

Philip Young, in his full-length study, attaches a

personal significance to Hemingway's concern with the death theme. Young suggests in Freudian terms that Hemingway suffered from a traumatic neurosis incurred by a severe wound in the First World War. As a means of adjusting to the neurosis, Hemingway acts under a "repetition-compulsion," which is the need to repeat an experience over and over. Hemingway's fiction, Young suggests, may be like Freud's war patients' dreams, in which the dreamers obeyed the repetition-compulsion, contrary to Freud's own notion of wish-fulfillment and the pleasure principle. More to the point, Young comments as follows:

> Hemingway — who writes, among other things, his nightmares — makes both simple and justifiable the identification of "fiction" with "dreams" here. Once this is done the theory fits and we put it on: suffering from the wounds and shock crucially sustained in the First World War, Hemingway, in terms of Freud's analysis, is continually in his prose disregarding the pleasure principle, and returning compulsively to the scenes of his injuries. He has his preoccupation with death as a result of an overexposure to it. . . . And that is not all: before Hemingway, symbolically through his hero, submits to this [regressive] drive he must occupy himself with vicarious dying —with witnessing and participating in many wars, many bullfights.[2]

In another and more recent full-length study, John Killinger, though repeating Carlos Baker and Philip Young on Hemingway's concern with death, refers to the Hemingway hero as one who has the existentialist pose.

Here then is the core of Hemingway's philosophy of violence: in the blinding flash of a shell, in the icy-burning impact of a bullet, in the dangerous vicinity of a wounded lion, in the sudden contact of a bull's horn, in that ill-defined twilight between life and imminent death where time and place are irrelevant questions, man faces his freedom. Nothing has any meaning at that instant except survival and existence. The superfluities of culture, race, tradition, even religion, all disappear in the face of one overpowering fact—the necessity to exist on an individual basis. This is the "separate peace," the only peace which can be won in our time.[3]

These and other commentaries indicate the importance of Hemingway's concern with death and violence. Whether his hero emerges with a healthy or sick mind, or whether he reflects an extreme individualism, can be judged only by examining the particular story in which he appears. What seems certain, however, is that Hemingway chose to focus upon these motifs as part of his attempt to explore the reactions of man under the pressures of the extreme in psychological and physical environment. The sequence of war stories exemplify this plan more pointedly perhaps than any other group, and the patterns which they formulate merge with the over-all theme of man seeking a way to adjust to the uncertainties of the world without losing himself in the process.

In the two stories entitled "Now I Lay Me" and "A Way You'll Never Be," Hemingway treats a young protagonist in the war. In the first the narrative identifies the character as "Nick," presumably Nick Adams. In the second he is identified as "Nick Adams," and most commentators consider that the same person is meant.

In the first the young protagonist might be characterized as having schizoid tendencies. As he lies in bed at night unable to sleep, a willful precipitation of regressive infantile reveries marks him as suffering from some acute mental disorder. Yet to rely solely upon such an explanation to supply the essential ingredients for the understanding of this piece is to miss the manifold suggestive possibilities which are employed by Hemingway to achieve certain artistic ends. To be sure, the whole work is suffused with psychological implications, and these are valid and important. Still, the technique of symbolization which incorporates these implications and charges them with meaning gives the story its artistic cast. By manipulating apparent devices in an inapparent manner, Hemingway takes what might have been a mere account of a battle-traumatized veteran and by adding scope and depth achieves an expansion of theme with universal implications.

The title, "Now I Lay Me," comes from the first line of the child's prayer,

> Now I lay me down to sleep;
> I pray the Lord my soul to keep.
> If I should die before I wake,
> I pray the Lord my soul to take.

The title as a correlative suggests an underlying irony which gives structural balance to the whole story. The opening line affirms this ironic function by echoing the title and localizing the action of the story. At the same time it adds a further detail which is in immediate discord with the initial correlative: "That night we lay on the floor in the room and I listened to the silk-worms eating" (363). The invocation of the silkworm image is the first of a series of repeated references to the worms, which soon begin to gather meaning in a symbolic context. The title is a rubric for the piece, and the silkworm references are related details which support the central drama of an intense inner struggle of a youth threatened with overwhelming regressive forces within his self.

The war experience provides the activating force for Nick's dream-like reveries. Traumatized by an initial encounter with death, he has become super-sensitized and cannot bear the analogous state of sleep: "I myself did not want to sleep because I had been living for a long time with the knowledge that if I ever shut my eyes in the dark and let myself go, my soul would go out of my body. I had been that way for a long time, ever since I had been blown up at night and felt it go out of me and go off and then come back" (363). The "flight of the soul" reference is a counterpoint to the second line of the child's prayer: "I pray the Lord my soul to keep." Nick's unwillingness to commit his soul to the care of divine authority is significative of his state of alienation and dissociation from the conventional sources of comfort and security. At the literal level the war wound precipitates the fear that the body will separate from the soul. But Hemingway invokes a second level of meaning. Since Nick reveals his plight of unfaith, the use of the term "soul" to depict his fear takes on secondary and ironically ambivalent associations. The central drama unfolding throughout the story becomes by this means a symbolic projection of his intense effort to reconcile within himself the dangerous tensions between the forces of chaotic instinctuality (war) and the forces of order and rationality (God). The fear of the loss of soul becomes the fear of the loss of God as a symbol of authority, law-giver, or orderer of the universe. In the reverie sequence Nick turns his thoughts to fishing and to his early family situation. Both incidents serve to illustrate dramatically a purposeful regression into an earlier period where peace and order were possible; yet his evident failure to assimilate and reconcile the disparate elements in his early environment parallels his present predicament.

In childhood "the God that failed" was, in fact, the boy's father, and the figure that emerged as the strongest force was his mother. In the normal adjustment to life, of course, the roles must be reversed. Once the child leaves the infant stage he must sever the umbilical cord of the protective sphere of the mother and advance into the world of the father. The father as authority figure, in his role as law-giver, forces the adjustment away from the protective womb and guards against the child's dangerous regressive tendencies. Recognition of the failure of the father at this point promotes regression. The child's failure to accept such a role in the father and reconcile himself to the life processes that role represents is tantamount to a direct denial of reality and a lapse into a fixed level of infantilism. Hemingway indicates that the latter was the case in the early life of Nick. The wound he received in the war recreates the adolescent experience of the first awakenings of knowledge of the dangerous, devouring aspects of the mother figure. The psychological symbolization becomes almost an equation: exposure to death *plus* fear of the womb (incest fantasy) *equals* fear of sleep (loss of soul). The whole equation rests upon the premise that the father, an authoritarian figure representing God, will fail to safely lead the individual through the trials to the threshold of individuation.

"I had different ways of occupying myself while I lay awake. I would think of a trout stream I had fished along when I was a boy and fish its whole length very carefully in my mind; fishing very carefully under all the logs, all the turns of the bank, the deep holes and the clear shallow stretches, sometimes catching trout and sometimes losing them" (363). This account by Nick depicts his attempt in reverie to recreate a world where order and reason are possible, as opposed to the chaotic and threatening world of reality. The description of the careful and methodic routine of fishing takes on an important ritualistic cast. As a conventional symbol of the Christian religion, fishing has connotations that are identical with those in the dream sequence. But it is not necessary to explore all the many harmonics in the symbolic spectrum to understand the implied meanings in the fishing imagery, for the language Hemingway chooses to illustrate Nick's feeling suggests a symbolic or ritualistic activity aiming at some redemptive response.

In the super-sensitive state in which Nick "fishes" at night, the peculiarities of ordered detail take on a significance beyond the ordinary. Part of the ritual of fishing includes a very careful testing and use of bait. In the context of the reverie the bait has sacrificial, associative implications: "Once I used a salamander from under an old log. The salamander was very small and neat and agile and a lovely color. He had tiny feet that tried to hold on to the hook, and after that one time I never used a salamander, although I found them very often. Nor did I use crickets, because of the way they acted about the hook" (364). As a fisher in the role of authoritarian law-giver, the dreamer cannot bear the vision of the salamander and cricket wriggling on a hook because their behavior is analogous to his own crucified state of hyper-sensibility. Even in the ordered realm of reverie the chaotic and instinctual elements of the irrational and unconscious impinge upon the dream of reconcilement.

The ever-present reflex of the dream of peace and security signals Nick's inability to assimilate the repressed elements within himself. He directly admits this failure in the context of his night "fishing" episodes, and the story transits into a further modulation of the regressive quest motif: "But some nights I could not fish, and on those nights I was cold-awake and said my prayers over and over and tried to pray for all the people I had ever known" (363-64). The expansion here to embody a vaster segment of humanity in his prayers reflects Nick's further identification with the Crucified One, Christ in Western culture. In particular, his inner determination is to identify himself with a broader contingent of humanity in order to assimilate to himself necessary bonds of attachment which will provide him with an identity, something his alienation and dissociation have taken away. His sought-for identity is not simply the lost old one; instead he is trying to establish a new identity in which he may become at one with the father. There is a parallel here to Christ crucified becoming at one with God the Father. And this instance is the basis for Christian martyrology.

As the narrative shifts into the new modulative level, the central character relates his attempt to recall his earliest experiences, "going back to the earliest thing you remember." Significantly, these early memories relate to the nursery drama: "the attic of the house where I was born and my mother and father's wedding-cake in a tin box hanging from one of the rafters, and, in the attic, jars of snakes and other specimens that my father had collected as a boy and preserved in alcohol, the alcohol sunken in the jars so the backs of some of the snakes and specimens were exposed and had turned white" (365). The obvious Freudian character of these notations seems hardly worth mentioning, yet the snake reference and its implication as a phallic symbol does have overtones in the archetypal drama that unfolds in the dream sequences. In association with the silkworm references and the reference to angleworms as bait, the snake image functions as a continuity in the symbolization, and a pattern develops. These biological images supply a common denominator to the individual referents, and a symbol of spiritual and moral atrophy emerges.

The fact that the snake is symbolic of the emasculated or ineffectual father is given further

credence when Nick reveals that these recalled objects
were stored in the attic of his grandfather's house.
The presence of the grandfather in this context implies that a surrogate father figure functioned for
the boy and temporarily postponed the trauma of
discovering the weakness of his natural father. When
the grandfather died, the family moved to a new
house designed and built by the mother, adding a
further detail to the portraiture of the weakling
father. The final and total destruction of the father
as symbol of authority and the clear emergence of
the mother as the dominant partner and victor over
the father is symbolized in the scene of what amounts
to a conflagration of the boy's world: "Many things
that were not to be moved were burned in the back-
yard and I remember those jars from the attic being
thrown in the fire, and how they popped in the heat
and the fire flamed up from the alcohol. I remember
the snakes burning in the fire in the back-yard"
(365). From then on the father has completely lost
his status. As Nick explains, "About the new house
I remember how my mother was always cleaning
things out and making a good clearance" (365).
Ultimately, the mother burns the father's prize collection of arrow-heads, the traditional symbols of
power and authority. The father's weak lament to
his son, "the best arrow-heads went all to pieces,"
reveals his own acceptance of defeat and acquiescence
in the passive role.

The sequential order of the narrative moves
next to a discussion of Nick's attempt to recreate the
story of Genesis in his realm of isolation. Having
considered his own childhood experiences and viewed

the far-reaching implications of the actions of both parents ("In remembering that, there were only two people, so I would pray for them both" [366]), and having explored the possibilities of effectual prayer ("Some nights, though, I could not remember my prayers even" [366]), he attempts to recreate his own identity by recreating the world of his past experience: "So on some nights I would try to remember all the animals in the world by name and then the birds and then fishes and then countries and cities and then kinds of food and the names of all the streets I could remember in Chicago, and when I could not remember anything at all any more I would just listen" (367).

When Nick reveals that "on this night I listened to the silk-worms," the symbolism of the "snake-worms" comes full around to signal a further modulative shift in the narrative pattern. The silkworm image has many suggestive possibilities, and one of the most important is the classical fate motif. The repeated reference to the noise of the worms eating operates at the auditory level and suggests the ever-present grinding of the wheels of fate, much as the classic chorus functioned in Greek tragedy. Hemingway takes advantage of the traditional usage, and the silkworms suggest the function of spinning, an analogy to the classical reference of the Fates: Clotho spinning the thread of life, Lachesis measuring it, and Atropos severing it.

The appearance of the silkworm image after the account of the dreams imparts meaning to the ironic correlative-prayer suggested by the title of the story, and it reinforces the theme of the destruction of the father figure carried through the sequence. This function is directly suggested when the story moves into its final modulation. Having related that on the particular night the story takes place another soldier is in the same room, Nick makes a telling comment: "but the silk-worms were not frightened by any noise we made and ate on steadily" (367). The apparent significance of the comment relates to what has come before. In spite of all his attempts at reconcilement, and in spite of all his appeals to discover a rationality that is operative in the universe, there is still an overriding "fate" which cannot be apprehended rationally. What Nick fails to see is that, as Hemingway has constructed him, he has already been victimized by the events of his early youth and by his failure to achieve a reconciliation with them. He is the picture of the traditional wounded hero languishing in the night-world, unable to reach the source of the healing, redemptive power.

The last section of the story points up Nick's final plight. Ironically, he is now at one with the ineffectual and emasculated father figure. John, the other soldier occupying the room, tells him, "You ought to get married. Why don't you pick out some nice Italian girl with plenty of money? You could get any one you want. You're young and you got good decorations and you look nice. You been wounded a couple of times" (370). John is married and has children, a natural state, and although he is sensitive he does not realize that the man to whom he is talking has had a much deeper psychic wound than decorations can ever signify. Nor does he realize that marriage for Nick is impossible. As a state of naturalness, it represents usurping the power of the father, a circumstance which is precluded because of the trauma that had its origins in the nursery intrigue.

"Now I Lay Me" points up much of Hemingway's ability to manipulate both psychological symbolism and conventional, representative symbolism. In part, this may be accounted for by a keen eye for suggestive detail, but the intricate patterns of symbolic equations that he consistently formulates as the central focus of the piece must be attributed to a careful and controlled attention to structural integrity. In "A Way You'll Never Be," he again deals with a protagonist caught in the plight of alienation and dissociation because of war, and the symbolism operates in much the same way. The literal manifestation of the plight of Nick Adams has been precipitated by a wound, but at the psychological level the configuration of details suggest more compelling psychic disturbances.

In a somewhat different manner than in "Now I Lay Me," Hemingway in "A Way You'll Never Be" treats the compulsive tendencies of an obviously "sick" hero. Although the two stories employ as protagonists characters who have been wounded in war and suffer deep underlying traumata, and although both "dream" while awake, the major similarity exists in Hemingway's treatment of the motif of adjustment to death and the ramifications of that theme. The whole of the dramatic action in "Now I Lay Me" takes place while the central character lies in his bed afraid of losing his soul in sleep, and the ensuing account is one of a waking-dream state. In "A Way You'll Never Be" the dramatic action follows a literal journey through a land that is suggestive of the trauma the protagonist has suffered. What is more, the narrative method differs in that "Now I Lay Me" is told in the first person, with the narrator relating in a self-analytic fashion his journey through certain major life experiences; in the other, "A Way You'll Never Be," the point of view is a central intelligence which objectifies the experience in the description of external realities away from the "sick" mind of the hero. This use of point of view is extremely important to the thematic emphasis of the story, for the tale is of an individual who is poised on the borderline of sanity and insanity, reality and unreality, and, ultimately, life and death. The point of view thus supports the central emphasis of the story by depicting both the inner thoughts of the character and the real world about him.

The framework of the conflict evolves from Hemingway's execution of the form of the story and his employment of at least the surface outline of the conventional journey motif. When Nick Adams is introduced at the beginning of the story, he arrives upon a scene of death and desolation caused by the war. The central intelligence describes in a matter-of-fact fashion the horrors depicted in the aftermath of a battle scene. The long descriptions and the cataloguing of the dead soldiers' paraphernalia is similar to the extended portrait of a battlefield in "A Natural History of the Dead," but here the scene serves to establish an important detail of setting which becomes the substructure of the whole story. The world to which Nick Adams has returned is the world of the dead. What follows the initial description of the land of the dead is a picture of a reality that is just as grotesque as this initial scene.

The central focus of the plot concerns Nick's visit to a battalion encamped along the bank of a river. The commander is an old acquaintance with whom Nick has endured many bitterly difficult war experiences. Nick has apparently just been released from a hospital after suffering a head-wound which has left him, as he puts it, "nutty." He has been returned to duty, but not as an ordinary soldier. He wears an American uniform, but it is one which has been tailored by an Italian and is "not very correct." His mission is to circulate through the Italian army and distribute cigarettes, postcards, and chocolate: "But there weren't any cigarettes and postcards and no chocolate" (406). Just as in several other stories, everything about Nick and the situation he is in suggests that something is slightly out of kilter.

As he becomes further involved in the action, it becomes evident that this is a journey of return for him. The places he passes, the landmarks he observes, and the meeting with his former soldier-comrade are all part of a world Nick has formerly been a part of in an intimate fashion. That he no longer belongs is apparent for many reasons, and his friend, Para, directly tells him to go back. In his response, Nick reveals his need to re-establish contact with the familiar in order to regain his former identity. " 'I heard the brigade was here so I thought I would see you or someone else I knew. I could have gone to Zenzon or to San Dona. I'd like to go to San Dona to see the bridge again'" (413). The bridge in this instance apparently holds some particular war memory for Nick, and his attitude evidences his compulsive need to revisit the scenes of his traumata.

Nick's periods of mental disorientation alternate with periods of complete rationality. When he has less lucid moments the innerworkings of his mind and his need to reconcile past trauma become evident, for his lapses function as an unconscious desire to create order out of his chaotic experiences. He "dreams" of the attacks in which he has participated, his experiences in Paris, and of fishing; at one point he attempts to explain to several Italian soldiers the habits and importance of the grasshopper. All of these relate to past, ordered experience. The "dreams" are purposeful in that they attempt to establish a re-orientation to the external world: "That was why he noticed everything in such detail to keep it all straight so he would know just where he was" (409).

The key repetitive image that occurs throughout the story is directly associated with Nick's need to reconcile the hurts suffered in his war experiences with his personal plight in the present. Hemingway graphically illustrates the extent to which the character has approached complete and final disorientation by the use of a triadic image. This is the image of a house, a stable, and a river. The first direct mention occurs when Nick "dreams" at the battalion headquarters.

> Sometimes his girl was there and sometimes she was with someone else and he could not understand that, but those were the nights the river ran so much wider and stiller than it should and outside of Fossalta there was a low house painted yellow with willows all around it

and a low stable and there was a canal, and he
had been there a thousand times and never seen
it, but there it was every night as plain as the
hill, only it frightened him. (408)

The image gathers meaning in the story context as
Nick continues the "dream": "He never dreamed
about the front now any more but what frightened
him so that he could not get rid of it was that long
yellow house and the different width of the river."
The final meaning emerges in light of the journey
motif: "Then where did he go each night and what
was the peril, and why would he wake, soaking wet,
more frightened than he had ever been in a bombard-
ment, because of a house and a long stable and a
canal?" (409).

Nick's journey back into the recesses of his mind
as a result of wounds suffered in the war is directed
toward a clarification of the processes of life and
death and the role the individual must play. In many
ways he is a kind of Lazarus who has returned. What
marks him as different from the biblical character is
that in his journey Nick has lost rather than gained
reconciliation. Death, insanity, and complete dissociation are still close at hand, as evidenced in his
"dream" of the house, stable, and canal. Both house
and stable are given a yellow color in the shifting
emphasis of the repeated image, and the river runs
"stiller" and "wider," depending upon how close he
is to a state of utter detachment from reality. These
are comforting and alluring manifestations of the
death state conjured up by Nick's unconscious, and
they suggest the pull toward total irrationality. For

him they are directly ambivalent in their connotations. He recognizes they are "what he needed," and still they frighten him. At one point they frighten him "especially when the boat lay there quietly in the willows on the canal" (408-09). This fear signals a very close proximity to total regression into the death-state, and the classical association with the river Styx and the boat provided for passage into the realm of death is evident.

Hemingway capsules the meaning of the images in a final dream sequence when the one-for-one relationship of the trauma Nick has sublimated into the triadic image is revealed: "He shut his eyes, and in place of the man with the beard who looked at him over the sights of the rifle, quite calmly before squeezing off, the white flash and clublike impact, on his knees, hot-sweet choking, coughing it onto the rock while they went past him, he saw a long, yellow house with a low stable and the river much wider than it was and stiller" (414). The direct identification of the recurring image with death as the result of a particular wound brings the thematic emphasis of the story into direct focus. Having made the journey of return to the scenes of his initial trauma, Nick can now make the association demanded by the dreams. Thus fortified, he is equipped to leave this symbolic realm of death and return to other pursuits. " 'I'm going, Para,' he said. 'I'll ride back now in the afternoon. If any supplies have come I'll bring them down tonight' " (414). But Nick has returned to this land in disguise, really, and the question of supplies — cigarettes, chocolate, and postcards — is a fiction. He has no function or purpose there any longer, for, literally, it is "a way he'll never be" again. He has reconciled himself to the knowledge of death, and any further return would be a useless repetition. He directly states his own positive step toward reconcilement to the Captain before he leaves: " 'You don't need to worry,' Nick said. 'I'm all right now for quite a while. I had one then but it was easy. They're getting much better. I can tell when I'm going to have one because I talk so much' " (414).

As Nick goes back, the central intelligence projects his thoughts, and all the images are peaceful and pleasant. The canal image is again mentioned, but in this context the victory over the forces it represents is apparent: "In the afternoon the road would be shady once he had passed the canal" (414). It also becomes evident at the conclusion that this is a new Nick, in the sense that he not only has overcome the possibility of slipping completely into the realm of regressive insanity but also that he has progressed beyond the stage of romantic notions concerning war. Passing a certain road in his projection of the return trip, he recalls: "It was on that stretch that, marching, they had once passed the Terza Savoia cavalry regiment riding in the snow with their lances. The horses' breath made plumes in the cold air. No, that was somewhere else. Where was that? 'I'd better get to that damned bicycle,' Nick said to himself. 'I don't want to lose the way to Fornaci' " (414). The emphatic rejection of the romantic in war concretely illustrates the change in Nick's personality. Although he still drifts from rationality, he does have control. He has essentially reconciled himself to his trauma by this return journey.

Perhaps a "message-hunter" might extract from "A Way You'll Never Be" the thought that Hemingway has said that "war is hell" or that it is "an insane affair." Both might be notions not too far from at least some of the implications. But in his symbolizations Hemingway employs a wide breadth of connotation, and the war theme is particularly suited to his purposes. Sometimes he takes the ramifications of his major themes and amalgamates them into seemingly simple and clear capsules that have no meaning beyond the obvious. Rarely is this the case, however, and when Hemingway does seem to be doing so one might well be suspicious and investigate beyond the surface. Two of his shorter pieces, "Old Man at the Bridge" and "On the Quai at Smyrna," belong in such a category. Each contributes some attitude or views in its own unique fashion some moment of war, and each provides adequate internal material to project the isolated theme into a more significant universal implication.

"Old Man at the Bridge" takes as its correlative and controlling symbol the tradition of Christ. The use of this device gives the piece a heavy cast of irony, and in so doing it purposefully demonstrates the disaster of contemporary man's loss of the Christian ideal. Hemingway's method of symbolization is rarely heavy-handed, though, and in this story the Christ reference is just barely perceptible. Yet it is there, and the technique of providing only the shadow of an outline of some conventional motif is one of Hemingway's important methods of amplifying simple, stark details into full-blown themes.

The plot outline suggests a rather sad account

of a very old man who is a refugee during the Spanish war. He has made it as far as a particular bridge, and the "I" of the story comes upon him and tells him to move on since the enemy will soon be upon them. After telling the "I" about some animals he has left behind in his home town, the old man tries to go on, but cannot. As the story concludes, the "I" relates the pathos of the old man's plight: "There was nothing to do about him" (80).

The old man here bears some resemblance to the hero of "The Capital of the World." Although the one is a young boy who has not experienced the "sophistications" of the large city and of life in general, both are pastoral types who are victimized by a society that is essentially corrupt. In this instance the corruption is illustrated by war rather than by psuedo-heroic bullfighters. The parallel is valid, however, for the same loss of the ideal which fostered the need for Paco to revalidate the Christian contract forces the old man to the brink of a similar fate. A like pressure causes the dissociation of the younger soldier-hero of "Now I Lay Me" and "A Way You'll Never Be." The implications of the loss of the ideal carry through to the "I" of this story, for the old man's presence forces an articulation of the pathos of the situation. This pronouncement by the narrator in the frame of the thinly outlined associations of the Christ motif gives this short, cryptic piece its universality.

From the very first mention the old man is a bit unusual. He wears "black dusty clothes" and has a "gray dusty face." The color and dust symbols are traditional; they suggest the association of the old man with death. He also wears "steel rimmed spectacles," a fact which suggests wizardry as well as perception. His repeated phrase, "I was taking care of animals," causes the narrator to acknowledge something unusual about him. "He did not look like a shepherd nor a herdsman," the narrator relates, and the old man supports these conclusions. " 'There were three animals all together,' he explained. 'There were two goats and a cat and then there were four pairs of pigeons' " (79).

The old man is not the center of attention in the story, however, for the attitudes of the narrator merge with the symbolic function of the old man and reflect the desperate spiritual plight of all men. Hemingway interweaves the surface suggestions of the old man's ensnarement with several pointed comments by the narrator in order to gain his purpose. After the narrator has questioned the old man when they first meet, he reports: "I was watching the bridge and the African-looking country of the Ebro Delta and wondering how long now it would be before we would see the enemy, and listening all the while for the first noises that would signal that ever mysterious event called contact, and the old man still sat there" (78-79). A subtle irony gathers meaning as the story progresses. The narrator is completely preoccupied with the coming of the enemy in the form of troops and war machinery, but "contact" has already occurred. When he encounters the old man, he has met with the more abstract but equally forceful manifestation of diabolic forces. The point becomes clear in light of the narrator's account of his mission: "It was my business to cross the bridge, explore the bridgehead beyond and find out to what point the enemy had advanced" (78). The meeting with the old man exactly relates the extent of the penetration of the "enemy," and the extent is that of the ideal of humanity and natural compassion — the pastoral ideal of the Christian faith.

The narrator does not apprehend that, embodied in the person of an old man caught in the trap of war, he witnesses the same symbolic drama he might have seen if he had been a Roman soldier at Calvary. Here the narrator is a soldier in the Spanish civil war, but the old man is not involved in the causes of the war. " 'I am without politics,' " he tells the narrator. In so doing he echoes the traditional posture of the Christ figure: "My Kingdom is not of this world." With the forceful entry of social contingencies into the pastoral world of the man who practices the ideal ("I was only taking care of animals"), on the wider scale of the symbolic interlude there is postulated the fate of those who cannot "adjust" — Crucifixion. Hemingway illustrates the kind of adjustment that is necessary in a world dominated by unpredictable evil in the reference to the animals the old man has left behind. For the pigeons, capable of flight, there is some little hope. The cat, the old man says, " 'will be all right. A cat can look out for itself, but I cannot think what will become of the others' " (79). The cat becomes the symbolic equivalent for the way to adjustment when the ordered pattern of existence has been reduced to chaos. Its characteristic detachment and aloofness, its natural equipment — teeth and claws — and the fact that it is a carnivore and predatory by nature, suggest the necessary emulation for the man who would survive in a world of contingencies. Goats, on the other hand, are a common sacrificial animal in mythology and the suggestion here relates to that source and function. The possible escape by flight of the pigeons, or, significantly in a biblical context, doves ("Did you leave the dove cage unlocked?" [80]), in terms of Christian symbolism would indicate that the qualities suggested by the Holy Spirit *might* suffice to effect an escape from the "enemy," but there is no assurance that they will.

Seen through the screen of the symbolic projection of traditional Christian lore, the full implications of this archetypal drama emerge in the final commentary by the narrator: "There was nothing to do about him. It was Easter Sunday and the Fascists were advancing toward the Ebro. It was a gray overcast day with a low ceiling so their planes were not up. That and the fact that cats know how to look after themselves was all the good luck that old man would ever have" (80). The reference to Easter Sunday points to the theme of Crucifixion, and the weather imagery reinforces the literal notation. The point is made that the weather, coupled with the full implication of the Easter reference, will not operate in favor of the forces of the "anti-Christ." For the moment, at least, complete mastery and domination by the "enemy" is forestalled. A point of irony supports the symbolic interplay in this connection. The soldier-narrator is a Loyalist, and the anti-clerical implications of that association would presumably preclude the possibility of his belief in the traditional Saviour. In a sense, then, as a representative of the

Loyalist ideal he personifies the anti-Christ. The encounter with the old man is in effect an ironic reversal. Although the narrator as a Loyalist is committed to the ideal of brotherhood, he cannot recognize the plight of the old man as that of everyman.

In such a context the full significance of the bridge as a symbol of the threshold between the forces of the pastoral, Christian ideal and those of the anti-Christ is revealed. The narrator has experienced a dramatization of the eternal struggle, and in his own personal role stands at the point of insight into this primal conflict. He cannot penetrate its significance, however, for he is blinded by the exigencies of the turmoil of his own isolated fears. He awaits a literal coming of an enemy, unaware that he has been provided a guide into the more profound ramifications of the entrance of evil into life. His final comment on the old man's "luck" reveals his own inability to accept the way of the ideal, and the conclusion reflects his own spiritual atrophy more than it does the plight of the old man.

Cast into the form of a story of utter simplicity, this piece crystallizes the effects of the irrational elements that constitute "war" on any level. In this sense no earthly protagonists are needed to give credence to the struggle. The conflict is an archetypal one, and the subtle interjection of key references of more than significative import is the mode by which Hemingway achieves an intense and amplified range beyond what might be expected from the narrative sparseness. Compacted and condensed allusions and imagerial references are carefully manipulated until they finally explode into universal themes. It is in the miniature drama form of the short story that tightly controlled artistry best achieves its ends, and in his short stories Hemingway exhibits this talent many times over.

"On the Quai at Smyrna" is another short sketch in which Hemingway demonstrates his ability to create expansiveness from scant narrative material. If the tale seems to represent the narrator's attitudinizing rather than characterize the effect of the war experience upon an individual, it is because the thematic overtones of the exhibited attitudes have been overlooked. The story is built on a juxtaposition of order and chaos, of natural and unnatural, and a tone of sophisticated irony dominates the narrative. The disastrous events of war reveal the true horror of unnatural adjustments and the insensibility of men. In a fashion that is often believed to characterize the Hemingway protagonist, the narrator of this piece opens with an apparently cold, objective, and aloof description of an event: "The strange thing was, he said, how they screamed every night at midnight." The clause "he said" indicates that the piece is being told secondhand by the narrator. This important fact cannot be overlooked in any discussion of this story, for the narrator might be ascribed attitudes which belong to the person who originally related the story from firsthand experience. Hemingway takes advantage of this rather subtle use of point of view by giving few indications that the direct observer of the incidents is not narrating the piece. Aside from the first line reference, there is one more "he said," and twice the person who tells the story addresses the narrator as "you": "*You* remember when they

ordered us not to come in to take off any more? . . .
You remember the harbor" (88, italics added). These
references argue for the narrator having been present,
but he never intrudes his own commentary upon the
story.

The narrative perspective in this story gains significance if one argues that this experience belongs
to the "generic Nick," and that the attitudes expressed are part of his loss of humanity at a particular juncture in his career. The notion of a generic hero
on its own grounds supposes a similarity in background and environment, which is always American.
Here, however, the character who is the storyteller,
as opposed to the narrator, is given obvious British
speech mannerisms. Several times he refers to "chaps,"
and at one point uses the phrase "most frightfully and
repeatedly insulting" (87). Again, at the end of the
story, in a telling display of attitude, he says, "It was
all a pleasant business. My word yes a most pleasant
business" (88). If the character were not British,
these ultra-sophisticated commentaries would not be
irony, they would be utter absurdities. The seriousness of the material and Hemingway's sustained pur-
posiveness would indicate them to be ironic.

From the opening lines the ironic juxtaposition
of details formulates the horror of the situation. The
use at the beginning of the third person pronoun "they"
to describe the unknown something or someone (as it
turns out, refugees waiting on the pier to escape) that
screams at midnight effects a depersonalization of the
nightmarish action. The next scene relates an incident
with a Turkish officer who is in a "frightful rage"
because he thinks he has been insulted by a seaman.

The subsequent polite and orderly attention to protocol
by the storyteller, in spite of the chaotic occurrences
around him, sets the tone and modulation of the story,
for it is this same unemotional attitude that is suggested
by the character's British mannerisms. Opposed to
such a reaction to the situation is the heroic posture
of the women refugees who will not give up their dead
babies. Their response is indicative of more than mere
surface sentiment; it is part of a compulsive desire to
cling to life. These bitterly natural reactions are in
contrast with the detachment affected by the observer-
participant.

The full irony of the story emerges in the para-
bolical commentary at the end: "The Greeks were
nice chaps too. When they evacuated they had all
their baggage animals they couldn't take off with
them so they broke their forelegs and dumped them
into the shallow water. It was all a pleasant business.
My word yes a most pleasant business" (88). The
plight of the mules becomes a parallel to that of the
people caught in the turmoil of war. Since the attitude expressed is not that of the actual narrator of
the story but of the observer-participant the suggestive irony is double-barbed. As part of the "rescue
force," the "I" reveals in his own attitude a commentary on the human situation. Trapped by forces beyond their control, crippled by their own keeper,
humanity is forced to rely on an indifferent rescuer.
Still, some hope remains, as evidenced by the women
who continue to propagate and protect their young
in spite of the chaos around them.

Hemingway's flair for the subtle cannot be ig-
nored in any of his work, for to overlook it is to miss

bolic and symptomatic of the unnaturalness of war.

This vast impersonality of war is ironically depicted in "In Another Country" by the "healing machines." They become synonymous with hope, healing, and even a kind of divinity. Hemingway uses the character of the doctor in the hospital to illustrate these functions. The doctor acts as a kind of healing-priest who derives his source of power from the machines. The war has disrupted the lives of those who are being treated in the hospital, and the resumption of their normal activities depends entirely upon the outcome of the treatment. The whole point concerning the machines is couched in irony, and this irony formulates the theme of adjustment.

The doctor has faith in the machines. When he asks the "I" what kind of sport he had participated in before the war and is told it had been football, the doctor expresses his confidence, telling him he will play again. The reality of the seriousness of the wound and the machines' ability to truly heal, as well as the doctor's romantic sentiments concerning his own ability to effect cures with the machines, is portrayed by the narrator's description: "My knee did not bend and the leg dropped straight from the knee to the ankle without a calf, and the machine was to bend the knee and make it move as in riding a tricycle. But it did not bend yet, and instead the machine lurched when it came to the bending part. The doctor said: 'That will all pass. You are a fortunate young man. You will play football again like a champion'" (268). The doctor's foolishness is never commented upon by the narrator; instead, this function is delegated to the Major who is taking treatments for a shriveled hand. He is the one who replies with sarcasm to the doctor's remarks to the "I," and in this way he effectively destroys the pose of the doctor as healer. "'And will I too play football, captain-doctor?'" The narrative then reveals that "he had been a very great fencer, and before the war the greatest fencer in Italy" (268).

With the introduction of the doctor and the Major into the narrative, the story has its full complement of characters for the symbolic drama which evolves from the contest between the doctor with his machines and the Major with his bitter creed of unfaith and detachment. The narrative "I" becomes the consciousness which observes the proceedings but which has already committed itself somewhat to the forces represented by the machines. The reason is given: "I was very much afraid to die, and often lay in bed at night by myself, afraid to die and wondering how I would be when I went back to the front again" (270). What is more, the "I" exhibits fears of being alienated from society, and the comradeship with the other wounded men is only a surface one. He explains the difference between them by use of metaphor: "The three with the medals were like hunting-hawks; and I was not a hawk, although I might seem a hawk to those who had never hunted" (270). The hawk which here has connotations of strength and purpose is also a predatory bird, and this suggests its ability to compete in a hostile environment. In spite of their characteristics, the three have been wounded, a fact which signifies the unpredictability of events regardless of one's ability to contend with environmental forces.

Hemingway has amply prepared for the conflict that emerges in the narrative, for in the opening paragraph certain details of setting appear which foreshadow the coming events: "There was much game hanging outside the shops, and the snow powdered in the fur of the *foxes* and the wind blew their tails. The *deer* hung stiff and heavy and empty, and small *birds* blew in the wind and the wind turned their feathers. It was a cold fall and the wind came down from the mountains" (267, italics added). The different attributes and modes of adjustment to the environment suggested by the game point to the plight of the soldiers who have been trapped in spite of their different qualities and backgrounds.

Exposed to the bitter attitudes of the Major, the narrator is still in touch with the romantic ideal. Assuming the role of tutor, the Major tries to teach the narrator the lesson of unfaith and detachment which will turn him away from that course.

"What will you do when the war is over if it is over?" he asked me. "Speak grammatically."

"I will go to the States."

"Are you married?"

"No, but I hope to be."

"The more of a fool you are," he said. He seemed very angry. "A man must not marry."

"Why, Signor Maggiore?"

"Don't call me 'Signor Maggiore.' "

"Why must not a man marry?"

"He cannot marry. He cannot marry," he said angrily. "If he is to lose everything, he should not place himself in a position to lose

that. He should not place himself in a position
to lose. He should find things he cannot lose."
(271)

The hospital becomes a substitute learning ground
for the narrator. Here he will learn of emotional
hurts which parallel and even surpass physical
wounds. The bitter attitudes of the Major challenge
the romantic notions he has retained. The sequence
resembles a teacher-pupil exchange, with the Major
attempting to instruct the narrator in the lessons of
unfaith. But as the narrator later learns, the words
spoken by the Major are prompted by the stress of
having lost his wife through sudden illness. Thus his
reactions are more emotional than rational, and the
weight of his argument is considerably reduced. The
Major is finally depicted as a weak and disillusioned
man. When he returns to the hospital, he admits the
failings of his own philosophical pessimism: " 'I am
utterly unable to resign myself' " (272).

A final irony is added to the inadequacy of the
Major's mode of adjustment, for when he returns
to the hospital he also returns to the machines. These,
too, are ineffectual, as he has already indicated, but
in his despair he commits himself to them and the
meaningless and hopeless ritual of exercise. The
pathos of the Major's capitulation is suggested by
the narrative tone: "In front of the machines the
major used were three photographs of hands like his
that were completely restored. I do not know where
the doctor got them. I always understood we were
the first to use the machines" (272). The ironic tone
suggests further that the narrator is himself cognizant

of the despair of the Major and the absurdity of believing in the machines. It is this recognition that marks a step toward insight for the narrator.

The narrator as central character is exposed to the two possible modes of adjusting to his own personal wounds and to the conflict implied in the knowledge that man is a victim of contingent forces. Hemingway does not suggest the final path the "I" chooses, for that is not the point of the story. He does, however, view the conflicting aspects of the Major's theories, for when put to the test they do not work. The role of the Major as tutor for the "I" breaks down, and this failure suggests that the ultimate discovery is that there is no single *way* to adjust. Words, creeds, and attitudes are reduced to absurdities in the face of the final test. The collapse of the Major and the narrator's empathetic response (" 'Oh —' I said, feeling sick for him. 'I am *so* sorry' " [272]) emerge as the only suggestion of an effectual way to deal with contingencies. The humanity of man is juxtaposed, finally, to the inhumanity of both the Major's attitudes and the forces represented by the machines.

War suggests in all these stories a process of dehumanization. The mode of survival, the real hope for man, always emanates from within individuals, and the response to be valid must be individual. A man's "road of trials" which he must travel throughout life is thus symbolized by the war-metaphor. Whether or not the particular protagonist is cognizant of the implications of his own isolated situation always depends upon his own strength of character. Few men are able to restore or find their own humanity under such stress. Hemingway does not aim to reveal man's continual victory over the forces represented by war, and neither does he aim to show man's continual defeat. These stories are portraits of man as an individual in conflict with overwhelming forces, and the reactions are those of man as a human being, not as a romantic caricature.

Leaving the war zone does not constitute leaving the implications of having experienced the strife of direct contact with death. Such an experience necessarily demands that an individual re-examine his old attitudes and beliefs and arrive at some new point of orientation. For a young man this discovery is particularly difficult, since it may mean the absolute destruction of all that he has been conditioned to believe since his birth.

The basic conflict aroused within the individual by such a situation is depicted in "Soldier's Home." As in many of the other stories, the title is an ironic commentary on the surface action. The "home" of the soldier in the story is not a place of comfort and security where a battle veteran may live out his life under the care of some benevolent agency. Nor is it a place where he may relax after the experiences he has undergone in the war. By virtue of having lived those experiences, he has lost all possibility of accepting the pressures and demands which once completely dictated the mode of his responses. The concept of home as a place of love also becomes a fiction, and the destruction of this notion as a value provides the impetus for the eventual severance from all that "home" represents. The central character of the story is Krebs, and he is the personification of man alienated from the traditional source of solace. Church, family, and society no longer command allegiance from the individual who has experienced the purgatorial initiation of war. "Home," as implied in the title, becomes the ultimate irony for Krebs, for it stands as a symbol of the stultifying pressures which emasculate the individual spirit.

The narrative follows a sequential pattern beginning with an authorial portrait of the central character. An interlude of action follows, in which the conflicts suggested in the portraiture are made evident. The concluding paragraph cites the resolution of the conflict within the character's mind. The form of the story allows Hemingway to achieve a depth in range of detail, although the dramatic time of the story proper covers only the few minutes it takes Krebs to arise, wash, shave, dress, and eat breakfast. The elapsed time is of importance to the central theme of the story, for the short span of time represents the character's "moment of decision."

The device of portraiture which Hemingway uses as the opening in the narrative divides into a description of two actual pictures and a representation of the background of the central character. The two pictures present a contrasting view of Krebs's life before the war and his life in the war. They foreshadow both the conflict and the resolution in the plot structure. The first suggests an ordinary young man committed to the conventions of his society.

> Krebs went to the war from a Methodist college in Kansas. There is a picture which shows him among his fraternity brothers, all of them wear-

ing exactly the same height and style collar. He
enlisted in the Marines in 1917 and did not return to the United States until the second division returned from the Rhine in the summer of
1919. (145)

The same flat atonality in the descriptive language
appears in the description of the second picture, but
there are several details which suggest that a considerable change has taken place in Krebs in the interval.

There is a picture which shows him on the
Rhine with two German girls and another corporal. Krebs and the corporal look too big for
their uniforms. The German girls are not beautiful. The Rhine does not show in the picture.
(145)

The second portrait illustrates pictorially the
effect of the war experiences upon the character. The
fact that he is in a picture with two German girls
and another corporal contrasts the foreign and different with the familiar of the first picture. Since the
two girls are "not beautiful," there is a hint that they
may not be the type with which a Methodist college
student would have associated. The ill-fitting uniforms
of both soldiers contrast with the collars of the fra-
ternity brothers. The conformity in style and height
in the first picture suggests the strict and stolid environment surrounding this brotherhood. The final
observation of the second picture which notes that
the Rhine river is not in the picture serves to illustrate
further that this scene is not intended to be suggestive

of the romantic notion of soldiers-of-fortune comfortably ensconced in an idyllic European setting.

As the narrative shifts to the authorial portraiture of Krebs, the implications of the second picture are reinforced: "By the time Krebs returned to his home town in Oklahoma the greeting of heroes was over" (145). The denial of status to Krebs by his society bridges the gap between the second picture and the dramatic present. The focus is then brought up to the point at which the story begins. The return portrays the isolation and separation of Krebs from those around him in much the same manner as the details of the picture taken during the war. He is forced to tell lies about his war experiences in order to gain the approval of his associates, but this fiction does not work. He cannot keep up the required pose: "Krebs acquired the nausea in regard to experience that is the result of untruth or exaggeration" (146). Krebs's reaction to falsehood points to the crux of his learning in the war.

The experience Krebs has undergone has had a cathartic effect upon him, and now that he has returned his actions are directly related to that war experience. Ironically, the home environment becomes the despoiler of his war-found individuality: "All of the times that had been able to make him feel cool and clear inside himself when he thought of them; the times so long back when he had done the one thing, the only thing for a man to do, easily and naturally, when he might have done something else, now lost their cool, valuable quality and then were lost themselves" (145-46). As in so many other Hemingway stories, the root of Krebs's conflict is grounded in the home environment. The attitudes of the members of his family toward his status as a returned soldier constitute a direct metaphor for the re-enaction of the triadic nursery conflict. Krebs's sisters form additional complements to the diverging forces. For them, Krebs is a hero. For the mother and father Krebs is still the same person who left to go to war. From the mother he receives attention of a sort, but she does not grant him the status of maturation: "She often came in when he was in bed and asked him to tell her about the war, but her attention always wandered" (146). The father, whose traditional role is that of guide into manhood for the son, fails to give his son the necessary posture of manhood: "His father was non-committal" (146). The errant and ineffectual father theme continues throughout the story and becomes the situational basis for Krebs's final denial of all authority.

One more facet of the conflict surrounding Krebs's return home is illustrated in the concluding portion of the authorial portrait. Krebs cannot engage in the societal intrigues of the community any more than those of the home. He feels the need for a woman, for example, but it remains in the realm of the abstract: "He did not want them themselves really. They were too complicated. There was something else. Vaguely he wanted a girl but he did not want to have to work to get her" (147). Any of the familiar attachments are "complications" for Krebs; his needs are sublimated into their ideational equivalent. But what has taken place is not simply an emotional dislocation in his character; it is a transference of his emotional center. As he emerges in the story action, this new orientation reveals his war-found moral center.

The opening narrative and dialogue passages of the section which begins the dramatic action reflect in capsular form the whole of the environmental pressures that impose themselves upon Krebs.

> One morning after he had been home about a month his mother came in to his bedroom and sat on the bed. She smoothed her apron.
>
> "I had a talk with your father last night, Harold," she said, "and he is willing for you to take the car out in the evenings." (149)

Krebs's reply to this statement of concession is cynical: " 'I'll bet you made him.' " The father no longer has any meaning as an authority figure, and his weakness is further revealed by the mother's attempt to strengthen him in order to serve her own ends. Her failure to recognize her son's change is apparent by her constant attempts to get him "to do" something. But Krebs is in open rebellion against all authority, and getting a job requires the kind of submission he cannot accept. By the end of the section he has systematically and completely rejected all conventional reflections of authority.

Initially Krebs denies the institutionalized religious authority to which his mother adheres. " 'God has some work for every one to do,' his mother said. 'There can be no idle hands in His Kingdom.' 'I'm not in His Kingdom,' Krebs said.' " Failing here, the mother then refers to the father as the authority: " 'Your father is worried, too.' " But "Krebs said nothing." Finally, unable to elicit the desired response by these appeals, the mother makes a direct appeal: " 'Don't you love your mother, dear boy?' " Krebs answers "No," and the subsequent, " 'I don't love anybody,' " marks the finale of his deliberately articulated rebellion (151-52).

By applying without limit the full range of the conventional symbols which ordinarily demand loyalty from the individual, the mother inadvertently forces Krebs into the decision he must make in order to reconcile his new self with the environmental situation. He must leave. When the mother makes her final plea, she reveals the "devouring-mother" aspect of her character. Krebs seemingly submits, but his own physical reaction indicates the incompatibility of such a submission. He "felt sick and vaguely nauseated" (152). Thereafter he goes through the form and even kneels to pray with his mother. The denouement relates his final decision, although his reactions have already indicated the necessary course he must follow: "He would go to Kansas City and get a job and she would feel all right about it" (153).

The theme of this story gathers symbolic value by means of its form. The story is not a simple growing-up story, even though it does have a close similarity to that formula. Hemingway works a variation by depicting a character who already has gone through a maturation process. The return home and the necessity to sever once and for all the restrictive bonds that stifle the moral impulse adds a new dimension. The return is a test for the central character. Had he failed to achieve a separation from the old authority figures, the formidable task of maturation already achieved in war would remain inconsequential. Krebs has won the right to individuality in the war, and he is his own man. The month he has spent at home signals the danger to his individuality, for the temptation to accept once again the old ways is compelling. Hemingway demonstrates the tension of the resultant conflict by means of a clear-cut division of the narrative. Krebs's surface reconcilement but personal moral outrage illustrate the forceful step he has taken toward individuation.

The return to the familiar environment also provides the surface plot outline for "Big Two-Hearted River." Both "Soldier's Home" and "Big Two-Hearted River" were written by Hemingway in the same year. The appearance of two stories with similar plots in a relatively short period would indicate the author's apparent interest at this time in the themes with which they deal. The basic situation that both consider concerns the vital adjustment processes an individual must undergo after he has been scarred by some great psychic shock. In Hemingway's treatment, however, there is a striking difference in methodology. In "Soldier's Home" the thematic content emerges essentially from the form of the story, and its prime expression issues through authorial or narrative revelation. This latter is coupled with a span of dramatic action which incorporates dialogue as its mode. Symbolic suggestion through literal detail is limited to brief descriptive "pictures" and to a rendering of key figures as symbolizations of the inner, compelling tendencies of the central character. In "Big Two-Hearted River" the mode of the story is expressed entirely through complex symbolic detail. The entire cast of the piece is suffused with the aura of the unreal, and Hemingway's ability to project the extreme conflicts of the protagonist through a screen of symbolization marks an elaborate and important dimension of his art.

Although Hemingway provides no internal evidence to suggest that the central character of "Big Two-Hearted River" has just returned from the war, quite obviously the character suffers from some great trauma that has occurred in his recent past experience. At least one of his symptoms is identical with that of Nick in "A Way You'll Never Be." Both have some mental disturbance that causes their minds to "work," a sign of the loss of control of the rational faculty. In this story, however, Nick refers directly to this kind of disturbance only once, and this recollection appears after he has gone through a whole ritual pattern of activity designed to prevent the loss of control it represents. The fact that "he could choke it because he was tired" indicates that he has conquered to some extent the dangers of complete irrationality.

The subject matter of this story concerns the particular activity of a fishing experience, and Hemingway manipulates the details of setting and character response in such a way that the experience becomes an attempt to recover psychic balance through a ritualization of a conventional activity. The need to restore this balance goes beyond the story itself, for Hemingway compresses into the form of the story the needs of generations of mankind to achieve a spiritual balance through ritual. The patterns of suggestiveness formulate in the character's spiritual dilemma the demands of forces beyond the immediate local situation. His apparent psychic shock over some trauma he has previously incurred and his strivings to overcome the residual effects of that trauma take for their example the archetypal conflicts of all men in their attempt to reconcile the existence of irrational forces in the universe. The fashioning of a panorama of symbolic projections of diverging forces indicates Hemingway's attempt to answer in kind the non-verbal, illusory fears which are part of the psychic make-up of all men.

Resting upon the "return to familiar ground" motif, the story generates within itself the motivation of the protagonist. This motivation becomes clear only obliquely, for it is never cited in any direct literal reference. The close focus of attention upon the slightest details points to a driving compulsion in the character to reaffirm the existence of order in the world. It is from this that the need to return springs. The journey back to a place where the need had been satisfied before the full knowledge that irrational forces operate in the world clearly prepares the way for the necessity of the subsequent ritual activity. The return in this story contrasts somewhat to the portrait of a visit to Italy taken by the two characters in "Che Ti Dice La Patria." The view exhibited there is one of suppressed violence. The war has laid the land waste, and for the people, whose moral state reflects the same "waste," there is no hint of a restoration.

From the opening lines of "Big Two-Hearted River" the landscape projects and catalogues the mental and spiritual plight of the protagonist. The setting into which he is first introduced is one where everything has been literally burnt to the ground. The settlement that once stood is now gone, and all that remains is the foundation of a hotel, "chipped and split by the fire" (209). If we accept the inferential thesis, the reflection here is a direct parallel to the psychic conflagration that has taken place within the character's mind. The shattering experiences of life have so afflicted him that all that remains of his former orientation to the world has been seared down to the base foundation of the self. The point of entry into the story is revealed in this manner, for the central character is to pass through a ritualized sequence of activity aimed at the restoration of the self. The story pattern, then, is an account of the protagonist's attempt to rebuild the necessary battlements of psychic balance which preserve the conscious self from total disorientation.

The reconstruction of the self through the return to the womb-like point of existence where security is guaranteed does not in itself constitute adjustment. The individual must achieve a genuine reorientation. For Nick this is so. Although he begins with slow stages of development, there is presented at least the possibility that he can eventually adjust. The narrative implies this recovery early in the story: "From the time he had gotten down off the train and the baggage man had thrown his pack out of the open car door things had been different. Seney was burned, the country was burned over and changed, but it did not matter. It could not all be burned. He knew that. He hiked along the road, sweating in the sun, climbing to cross the range of hills that separated the railway from the pine plains" (210-11). At the psychological level, the fact that it makes no difference about the town, the old self, is indicative of the need to recreate the self based on what has gone before. To simply restore the old would be to subject it to a repetition of the conflagration. To rebuild a new self out of the old self is to structure a much stronger edifice.

The division of the story into Part I and Part II reinforces the implications of the return motif. The first part reveals the details of the preparation for the meaningful experience which will mark the reconstruction of the self. The second part deals with initiatory rites that test the ability of the new to withstand the symbolically reflected catastrophies of life.[4] Significantly, Hemingway employs the controlling symbol of water, the Black River, to suggest the revitalizing forces surrounding the rebirth of the self. The color name of the river suggests, too, the dangers inherent in the return, for if the individual were not in imminent danger of regression or total disorientation he would not have progressed to the point where a rebirth could be achieved. The river as symbol implies the possibility of revitalization at one extreme but absolute destruction at the other.

Nick's journey toward a "good spot" for fishing along the river parallels the traditional references to myths of rebirth. He must endure the pain of his own burden to get beyond the isolated and local to the area where spiritual resuscitation is possible: "The road climbed steadily. It was hard work walking up hill. His muscles ached and the day was hot, but Nick felt happy. He felt he had left everything behind, the need for thinking, the need to write, other needs.

It was all back of him" (210). The burden Nick carries here is revealed quite literally, and it pertains to the need for the return. "Thinking" is significative of the protagonist's plight, for this is the process which recalls those past experiences which are too destructive to normality to dwell upon. The point is that the character must force his mind to occupy itself with other matters, regardless of the pettiness of their nature. It is the form, not the content, which becomes the saving grace. Here the preoccupation is with fishing, and the minutiae surrounding the simple experience takes on a therapeutic meaning.

In Part II, having established his camp, Nick is poised for the vital moment of the symbolic ordeal. Hemingway portrays the mental and spiritual conflict of the character by employing a triadic symbolization of its content: "There was the meadow, the river and the swamp" (221). The meadow suggests the secure, protective agency at the point of suspension between past traumata and future life. To live in a sunny meadow all day, however, is a denial of life, for the road of trials demands involvement in life's complex. The river suggests an involvement in "the stream of life," as it were, and beyond that stands the swamp, the unknown. The life processes terminate in this unknown, and ultimately Nick must face this reality. Hemingway reflects this in his account: "Ahead the river narrowed and went into a swamp" (230).

As the action continues, Nick moves out of the meadow into the stream. That this movement is the equivalent to the immersion back into some life stream is signaled by the descriptive account: "He stepped into the stream. It was a shock. His trousers clung tight to his legs. His shoes felt the gravel. The water was a rising cold shock" (224). The shock of this baptismal-like re-entry reveals the ultrasensibility of the character. The first shock over, he fishes the stream. Each detail of the bait, casting, and landing of several trout is minutely described. Finally the "big fish" is hooked, but it escapes. This elicits a peculiar reaction: "Nick's hand was shaky. He reeled in slowly. The thrill had been too much. He felt, vaguely, a little sick, as though it would be better to sit down" (226). The nausea in this instance is a reflection of the encounter with powerful forces of the unknown, for this is a direct encounter with the reality Nick had sought to escape. But Nick does recover, and this renovation points to a stage in his readjustment. The narrative directly suggests that this trout is not an ordinary fish Nick has hooked, at least not to him in his hypersensitive state: "He had never seen so big a trout. There was a heaviness, a power not to be held, and then the bulk of him, as he jumped" (226).

Nick recovers from the encounter. The narrative indicates that he has proceeded to a further stage of adjustment: "It went away slowly, the feeling of disappointment that came sharply after the thrill that made his shoulders ache" (227). The fish as symbol begins to ramify in this context until it finally stands for the entire purpose of Nick's effort. His striving to catch the "big fish," its escape, and his "nausea," and his slow reconcilement project Nick's struggle to gain some hold on reality. At the same time Nick accepts the existence of unknown powers.

The swamp is the habitat of the "big fish," and Nick must at some time squarely face the unknown it represents. But Nick realizes he is not ready for the total effort. Rather than emerging as the man who has found himself, he is in a stasis as one who, having taken a step toward individuation, wishes for time to adjust to an overwhelming change whose meaning is not yet clear.

> Nick did not want to go in there [swamp] now. He felt a reaction against deep wading with the water deepening up under his armpits, to hook big trout in places impossible to land them. In the swamp the banks were bare, the big cedars came together overhead, the sun did not come through, except in patches; in the fast deep water, in the half light, the fishing would be tragic. In the swamp fishing was a tragic adventure. Nick did not want it. He did not want to go down the stream any further today. (231)

Realizing his own limitations, Nick resolves his immediate difficulties. In the line of the story the major step is directly related to the possibility of complete reconciliation and final emergence of a man who has attained selfhood: "There were plenty of days coming when he could fish the swamp" (232).

Chapter VI

The Marriage Group

AMONG HEMINGWAY'S SHORT STORIES are a number which deal with the theme of love-relationships between men and women. In most the marital tie is the focus, but there are several which go outside the conventional and examine events arising from the extra-marital association of two people. Usually these fictions are short, rather terse accounts of some particular event which reflects a mood of estrangement and alienation. Several longer stories deal with similar themes, but, generally, as in "The Short Happy Life of Francis Macomber" and "The Snows of Kilimanjaro," the isolation of an individual because of marital difficulties is not the central purpose of the story. In these and other stories with a major portion of the action involving war, bullfighting, or some sport, the nature of the subject matter is such that it charges the situational conflict with hyperbolic force. Characters are thrust into broad relief by their responses to their circumstances. In the marriage stories no such inner force is derived from subject matter, and Hemingway must accomplish his ends by the use of other means. Sometimes he creates tension between the major participants in the action; at other times he uses subtle irony. Occasionally he devises special effects to point to his theme. Even in the instances where the plot and theme seem trivial, Hemingway clearly strives to portray a facet of man's never-ending struggle to come to terms somehow with the world he faces.

Of the many methods Hemingway chooses to depict his characters, placing them in ironic circumstances is among the most important. Always these situations presage a conflict of values in a world where the moral substructure has been undermined. The marriage situation in its implication of a union of two individuals implies action in the moral sphere. When something goes wrong in this smallest of social units where morality operates, any deviation has repercussive effects which swell and encompass the entire societal organism. The union of two individuals demands that both participants have progressed beyond the ego-centered interests of childhood and adolescence. If either has not, the resultant conflict may take on gigantic proportions with sinister implications. Such is the situation in many of the marriage stories, and the importance of the focus goes beyond mere marital disturbances; it reflects a sickness in a culture where man is barred from the natural sources of vitality. The sickness is a moral one, and the characters are not so much victims as conspirators. The stories which fall naturally together as the direct expression of the marriage metaphor are "Mr. and Mrs. Elliot," "Cat in the Rain," "Out of Season," "Hills Like White Elephants," "A Canary for One,"

"The Sea Change," "A Very Short Story," and "Homage to Switzerland."

In "Mr. and Mrs. Elliot" the ironic tone keys the drama of sexual sterility to such a pitch that the resultant implosive accumulation of detail stereographically shapes a portrait of the moral and spiritual impotence of the central characters. These people are more caricatures than characterizations, for they personify attitudes and responses more than they do individuals with a wide range of human attributes. Never do they emerge as important for their own sake, and yet this shallowness does not detract from the impact of the story. As part of Hemingway's design, the method of the story is strictly narrative. This varies somewhat from his conventional mode of structuring the short stories, but, as his narrative pattern amply illustrates, the structure is aimed directly at creating a particular effect upon the reader.

The opening line of the story establishes the fundamental situation around which the whole of the action takes place: "Mr. and Mrs. Elliot tried very hard to have a baby" (161). As the narrative unfolds, the full ironic implications of this initial statement are revealed. The interpretation is signaled by the use of a key word which by its repetition becomes the narrative comment upon the relationship between the two characters: "Mrs. Elliot was quite *sick*. She was *sick* and when she was *sick* she was *sick* as Southern women are *sick*" (161, italics added). The "sickness" goes beyond mere physical discomfort. As other factors of this marriage are related, it soon becomes apparent that there is an abnormality within the individual characters. The fact that Elliot at twenty-five has married a woman of forty suggests what becomes apparent later in the narrative — his outsized mother complex — and what the people on the boat to Europe observed when they "took her for Elliot's mother" (161). The effects in Elliot of the refusal to sever the childish ties to his mother are further illustrated by the narrative account of his notions of purity: "He wanted to keep himself pure so that he could bring to his wife the same purity of mind and body that he expected of her. He called it to himself living straight" (161). In a conventional frame the attitude in itself might seem noble, but the narrative suggests further that this manifestation reflects a prudish streak in Elliot: "He was shocked and really horrified at the way girls would become engaged to and marry men whom they must know had dragged themselves through the gutter" (161-62).

Elliot's "purity" is lauded by his wife. Her response, "You dear sweet boy," suggests that she views their marriage more as a mother-son relationship than that of man and wife. When the couple arrives in Europe the situation deteriorates completely. Mrs. Elliot prevails upon her husband to send for her "girl friend" from Boston, and with the arrival of this character the central focus of the story shifts into a commentary upon the adjustment to abnormality. The concluding portion of the narrative suggests more than it says of the nature of this adjustment.

> Elliot had taken to drinking white wine and lived apart in his own room. He wrote a great

deal of poetry during the night and in the morning looked very exhausted. Mrs. Elliot and the girl friend now slept together in the big medieval bed. They had many a good cry together. In the evening they all sat at dinner together in the garden under a plane tree and the hot evening wind blew and Elliot drank white wine and Mrs. Elliot and the girl friend made conversation and they were all quite happy. (164)

The complete reversal of normal roles becomes the point here, for the action has come full cycle from the opening line. There Mr. and Mrs. Elliot are said to be trying to have a baby; here the suggestion is quite clear: Mrs. Elliot, at least, has got her baby — Mr. Elliot. The implied abnormal relationship between Mrs. Elliot and the girl friend, who is "several years older," is one in which the girl friend has become a surrogate husband. Now the controlling figure of the complex, she has usurped Elliot's marital bed. Elliot's poetry has become his substitute mate; his sleeping apart and working at night suggest that it has become a substitute for the sexual act. The evening scenes typify a normal family setting, but here it is presented in ironic terms. The girl friend and Mrs. Elliot engage in "conversation" (an obvious pun on the archaic meaning of the word), and this is an adult function. Elliot drinks white wine, a fact which suggests milk or some other innocuous or soporific beverage. In this way Elliot's lapse into a childish state is portrayed, and he never does become a man or its equivalent: "get a baby."

Essentially, Hemingway effects a reduction of

the characters into burlesque caricatures of themselves, but their responses are veracious in that they
are consistent with their own shortcomings. Elliot's
actions in particular reveal an important point about
Hemingway's view of the hero: Elliot fails to fulfill
himself and separate from the maternal cord. His
refusal directly results in the final regression into
which he lapses. The adjustment, in this instance away
from reality, is the mark of a character type who
appears both in the stories and in the longer fiction.
Each time this figure appears he not only illustrates
a failure to adjust to the vicissitudes of the world
but also a failure even to strive. Hemingway's tone
in the treatment of such a character is always heavily
ironic and scornful, for failure to strive represents for
him the most abysmal sterility.

In "Cat in the Rain," Hemingway uses the slight
instance of a woman's seeing a cat outside her hotel
window as a springboard for the expression of the
basic needs of individuals. The setting initially establishes the tone and mood of the piece in a pictorial
manner. The husband and wife here are Americans
living in an Italian hotel which faces the sea, a public
garden, and a war monument. It is raining and the
square is empty of people. The emphasis of the narrative is on the loneliness and forlornness suggested by
the rain: the war monument "was made of bronze
and glistened in the rain. It was raining. The rain
dripped from the palm trees. Water stood in pools
on the gravel paths. The sea broke in a long line in
the rain and slipped back down the beach to come
up and break again in a long line in the rain" (167).
The doleful tone invoked by the rain and sea imagery

foreshadows the coming action on the surface level and suggests the inner conflict of the chief character. When the woman sees the cat outside in the rain "trying to make herself so compact that she would not be dripped on" (167), the first stage of a projection of her inner feeling onto an exterior element begins.

Hemingway's ends are served in this story by the use of irony. When the woman goes after the cat, she encounters the hotelkeeper, a personage who becomes for her a substitute authority figure. Her reaction to him reveals that in this guise he assumes a benevolent role: "He stood behind his desk in the far end of the dim room. The wife liked him. She liked the deadly serious way he received any complaints. She liked his dignity. . . . She liked the way he felt about being a hotel-keeper. She liked his old, heavy face and big hands" (168). The characteristics the woman notes and "likes" in the hotelkeeper indicate that what she really sees in him is a reflection of the father *imago*. That is, she sees a projection because of her own inner need to identify herself with someone who seems to conform to her notion of what a benevolent and protective father ought to be, not what a father is really likely to be. In her fantasy she is not totally unlike the girl in the sketch "One Reader Writes." The character there sends a letter to a doctor in the hope that he can advise her whether she can "live" with her husband who has contracted "sifilus." In her absolute ignorance and remorse, the girl resorts to faith in an anonymous "god-doctor" figure who appears in a newspaper. The irony of her pathos is revealed in the last lines of the sketch: "I wish to Christ he hadn't got any kind of malady. I don't know why he had to get a malady" (421).

The hotelkeeper in "Cat in the Rain" reinforces the myth of his aloof benevolence by sending a maid with an umbrella along with the woman so that she will "not get wet." That the wetness signifies more than rain becomes increasingly apparent as the story progresses, and so does the woman's identification with the cat. While they are outside looking for the cat, the maid asks the woman the meaningful question: "Ha perduto qualque cosa, Signora?" (Have you lost something, Madame? [168]). Within the narrative structure the question becomes the point of the whole story. What the woman has lost is something she herself cannot readily articulate, although later she does approach articulation in a plea to her husband.

Part of what the woman has lost is the intimacy with her husband which would shield her from insecurity. Hemingway portrays her isolation by means of the husband's responses. When she returns to the room, her husband does not see that she has identified with the cat: " 'Wonder where it went to,' he said." Her reply suggests her identification: " 'It isn't any fun to be a poor kitty out in the rain'" (169). As the narrative progresses the woman more pointedly tells her husband of her inmost desires:

> "I want to pull my hair back tight and smooth and make a big knot at the back that I can feel," she said. "I want to have a kitty to sit on my lap and purr when I stroke her."
> "Yeah?" George said from the bed.

"And I want to eat at a table with my own silver and I want candles. And I want it to be spring and I want to brush my hair out in front of a mirror and I want a kitty and I want some new clothes." (169-70)

In his detachment the husband cannot understand that her desires are expressions of certain inner needs, and all he can suggest is a substitute: " 'Oh, shut up and get something to read' " (170).

The final irony of the narrative occurs at the conclusion, and it comes in the guise of the maid: "In the doorway stood the maid. She held a big tortoise-shell cat pressed tight against her and swung down against her body. 'Excuse me,' she said, 'the padrone asked me to bring this for the Signora' " (170). The gift of the cat is an answer to the literal, superficial need of the woman but in no way answers the greater needs suggested by her identification with the cat that had been outside. The husband's failure as the spiritual provider is now paralleled by the hotel-keeper's failure. Having projected onto this personage the characteristics of an authority-provider, or father, her final disillusionment, ironically, comes about by the nature of the gift.

The failure of individuals to sustain the role into which they have been cast, or, ultimately, the failure of all authority to provide meaningful guidance, implies a commentary beyond the literal. In both this story and in "Mr. and Mrs. Elliot" the failure is the mechanism of the story structure. But in Hemingway's treatment of love-relationships, one of the individuals may not fulfill the promise of love as well. This failure often provides the mechanism for a portrayal of the inability to adjust to the contingencies of the life situation. The young man in his attempt to reach maturity and cast himself in the role of father-authority may encounter many rebuffs along the way. His acceptance of such denials would indicate the real level of maturation he has achieved. Many times, however, he cannot, and such a development provides a point of conflict. In "A Very Short Story" Hemingway illustrates the effects of the withdrawal of the promise of love upon a young man who has just returned from war.

The story is actually a vignette written as a straight narrative account. As such it is not intended to dramatize the many ramifications a love conflict may imply. Rather, the piece is more of a capsule portrait of a love affair that is not fulfilled. The simple plot outline concerns a young soldier who has an affair with a nurse in a hospital where he is receiving treatment — the germ of a part of *A Farewell to Arms*. The affair becomes serious and, after the armistice, they decide to marry when he returns home and gets a job. The girl, Luz, remains behind to wait. After he is gone, however, she writes to him and tells him that she has changed her mind because "she realized now it was only a boy and girl love" (142). She tells him that she will soon marry an Italian officer, and thus the affair is terminated.

The effect of such a severance is related in ironic terms: "The major did not marry her in the spring, or any other time. Luz never got an answer to the letter to Chicago about it. A short time after he contracted gonorrhea from a sales girl in a loop department store while riding in a taxicab through Lincoln Park" (142). The ironic tone indicates the commentary. The withdrawn promise of love has reduced the ideal of a love-relationship for the young man to mere sexuality. Luz's apparent hint of the possible re-establishment of the old ties — she writes to him about the end of the other affair—cannot be accepted by him. The original hurt of the denial of his role — "a boy and girl love" — has apparently forced him into an adolescent regression and consequent denial of what he had experienced while at the hospital. For him the original failure of the love-partnership is reflected as both a physical and psychological disease.

A somewhat similar failing provides the commentary upon the thematic content of "Out of Season," another marriage story. The title of this story itself functions significatively. Literally it refers to trout fishing, but at another level it applies to the disenchantment with the love-relationship between a husband and wife.

The abortive fishing excursion which is the subject of "Out of Season" provides the metaphorical basis for a complicated joke in the narrative. This comes about by Hemingway's use of materials seemingly external to the central situation, but he so fuses these materials with the thematic content that the end result is a single, overall effect. The chief characters involved in the fishing episode are "a young gentleman," his wife, and Peduzzi, a drunken Italian guide. The focus is primarily upon the husband, who is to be the fisherman in this "out of season" excursion. The basic situation involves no more than the fact that Peduzzi has interested the husband in some illicit trout fishing. The wife has many reservations about the venture and turns back before they reach the river. When the husband and Peduzzi reach the river, they find that they cannot fish because they have no lead sinkers. The heavy irony throughout cannot at times be distinguished from outright joke; yet it is this particular feature that gives the story its real meaning.

Throughout the story the reference to the husband as a "young gentleman" is repeated a sufficient number of times until it finally assumes a meaning beyond literal notation. What it becomes is an ironic tag-name to represent the inner weaknesses of the character. His guide, Peduzzi, also bears a name which is ironic within the story context. His name suggests "teacher," but what he has to teach is neither legally nor morally wholesome or desirable. His own character is reflected by his occupation, which includes "breaking up frozen manure with a dung fork" (179). As a guide he is a mock-figure. What his guidance leads to is illegal fishing in a "brown and muddy" river with a "dump heap" nearby. The association of the "young gentleman" with Peduzzi illustrates by ironic contrast the degeneration of values within the character; yet the break away from Peduzzi at the end of the narrative does not necessarily imply a regaining of lost values.

The joke of the story enters at that point in the narrative when the characters are en route to the river. In an attempt to inveigle the husband out of some wine for himself, Peduzzi suggests that they buy some marsala "for the *Signora*." The wine reference causes the husband to reflect on a point seemingly outside the bounds of the narrative: "The young gentleman appeared not to hear Peduzzi. He was thinking, what in hell makes him say marsala? That's what Max Beerbohm drinks" (174). The reference does have importance. An English writer, Beerbohm produced works that were characterized by a certain degree of preciosity and gentlemanliness, and Hemingway apparently objected to it. The cutting remark forces the reader into a closer consideration of its occurrence. In order to leave no doubt that the comment is meant as a slight, Hemingway puns on the next word. The pretext for the pun is Peduzzi's attempt "to bring the young gentleman into action": "'Geld,' Peduzzi said finally" (174). Suggesting castration as well as money, the pun appearing just after the Beerbohm reference further personifies the type of individual the husband has become.

The difficulty between the husband and wife also takes its meaning within the suggestive range of the pun on castration. The precise nature of their own problem is never revealed directly, but in the single instance when the friction becomes overt the wife's mockery implies there is something wrong in the love-relationship.

> "I'm sorry you feel so rotten, Tiny," he said.
> "I'm sorry I talked the way I did at lunch. We were both getting at the same thing from different angles."
> "It doesn't make any difference," she said. "None of it makes any difference."

"Are you too cold?" he asked. "I wish you'd
worn another sweater."

"I've got on three sweaters." (175)

The wife's final comment suggests that the discord
lies in the area of sexual estrangement or incompatibility. At any event, it portends a coming greater
disharmony and conflict.

The husband's weakness of character is further
thrown into relief by another comment the wife
makes. When he worries about having been seen
carrying the rods through the town, she scornfully
rebukes him: " 'Of course you haven't got the guts
to just go back. . . . Of course you have to go on' "
(176). The husband's fear of the authority of the
"game police," along with his insistence on continuing at all events, is a reflection of his struggle
to emerge as a man from the role of "gentleman"
he has been playing. In his relations with his wife
and with Peduzzi he is a victim of his own weakness.
He cannot face the scorn of the wife, nor can he
refuse Peduzzi's suggestion to fish illegally. For him
the fishing expedition becomes an outward token of
his inner rebellion. In this light Peduzzi functions by
way of double irony. He is both a mock-figure and
ineffectual guide, but at the same time he represents
for the husband the opportunity to leap the bounds
of legal and social authority and achieve some individuality.

The husband's tentative step in the direction of
rebellion is finally a failure. This is illustrated by a
further reference to the castration metaphor. He
cannot fish because he has no "lead." The prophetic

words come from Peduzzi: "'You must have some lead.' Peduzzi was excited. 'You must have piombo. Piombo. A little piombo. Just here. Just above the hook or your bait will float on the water. You must have it. Just a little piombo'" (177). Peduzzi's plea goes unacknowledged, however, for the man has no "lead," literally. The double-entendre here in its second meaning refers directly to the man's lack of vitality. The phallic suggestivity of the fishing rods further supports the implications of the second meaning, and both echo the Beerbohm reference and pun on "Geld." In essence, ironically enough, Peduzzi becomes the commentator who disparages the character and courage of the husband. In this way the weaknesses of this individual are illustrated by the narrative joke.

The moral cowardice of the husband provides the basis for the seeming change in his character at the end of the story. After it is decided they cannot fish, "the young gentleman felt relieved. He was no longer breaking the law" (178). Peduzzi, however, still insists that they return the next day, and the husband's response is indicative of his inability to exert himself as an individual. By association he is equated with Peduzzi, and both are pictured as the lowest of the low: "'Thank you, *caro*. Thank you,' said Peduzzi, in the tone of one member of the Carelton Club accepting the *Morning Post* from another'" (179). The young man makes a feeble attempt to extricate himself from the association, but his method illustrates his cowardice as much as the association. He tells Peduzzi he does not know whether they will fish together the next day, but he "will leave word with the padrone at the hotel office" (179). He still cannot accept responsibility directly, and therefore he appeals to a buffer authority figure.

This story at one level may well be a commentary by Hemingway upon his contemporaries, but this is of no great consequence to his treatment of the theme of individuation. What is important in this respect is that the story formulates a portrait of an individual who is simply too weak to undergo any vital experience. He is not too different from Mr. Elliot, for neither is able to overcome adult complexities. The husband becomes involved in a childish rebellion against authority, but his failure to step beyond the line clearly marks an inner immaturity and inability to face reality directly.

The refusal to recognize and accept the natural processes of life is again demonstrated in "Hills Like White Elephants." The woman here is pregnant, and the man cannot accept the complications this must necessarily bring about. His refusal is not portrayed as a simple, crass unfeeling; it is, as he views it, that the child will impinge upon his freedom. The irony of the narrative is based upon this notion, for, as the woman suggests to him, the child would not abort his freedom but would grant him "everything." The man's refusal to admit the efficacy of the normal processes reflects an ego-centered, adolescent attitude within him and establishes him as one of the many emotional and spiritual cripples within the "marriage group."

The details of setting in the story become an external reflection against which the remarks and attitudes of the woman gather implicit meaning. The initial details establish the basic metaphor: "The girl was looking off at the line of hills. They were white in the sun and the country was brown and dry. 'They look like white elephants,' she said" (273). From this first identification, the term "white elephant" becomes metaphorically an objectification of the inner conflict. The man wishes her to have an abortion, and at the first level the child is the "white elephant." Hemingway plays on the term, however, for a "white elephant" by definition has several implications. It not only means an annoyingly useless gift; it may also be a possession of great value. In this context the child symbolizes the husband's inability to see that the child might provide a meaning to life which he lacks.

The details of setting contrast the sphere of sterile unfeeling with that of the life which incorporates the natural processes. By employing these details in establishing the fundamental situation, Hemingway presents the line of demarcation between the world of the man and the world of the "white elephant":

> The hills across the valley of the Ebro were long and white. On this side there was no shade and no trees and the station was between two lines of rails in the sun. Close against the side of the station there was the warm shadow of the building and a curtain, made of strings of bamboo beads, hung across the open door into the bar, to keep out flies. The American and the girl with him sat at a table in the shade, outside the building. It was very hot and the express from Barcelona would come in forty minutes. It stopped at this junction for two minutes and went on to Madrid. (273)

Several factors here are important to the symbolization. The dramatic time is given, so the whole of
the action is telescoped into "forty minutes." Placing
the action in the waiting room of a train station, and
having the characters awaiting a train which will stop
for only two minutes, provides an intense focus upon
the decision to be reached by the characters in the
short span of time available. The details of sun and
shade, of heat and relief from heat, of barrenness and
vegetation contrast the train station where the action
takes place with the hills in the distance across the
river. Since the hills are identified with the "white elephant" symbol, the contrast and identification solve
the symbolic context. The child, like the opposite side
of the valley, represents fructification.

Hemingway reinforces the contrasting details
throughout in order to establish a symbolic valence
for each rather than simply to give them signific
identification. At a crucial point in the narrative,
for example, he identifies the desire of the woman
to have the child and lead a life of normality with
the hills and valley — the region of fecundity: "The
girl stood up and walked to the end of the station.
Across, on the other side, were fields of grain and
trees along the banks of the Ebro. Far away, beyond
the river, were mountains. The shadow of a cloud
moved across the field of grain and she saw the river
through the trees" (276). The sympathetic relationship established between the woman's inner yearnings
and the external setting prepares the way for her
direct articulation of the meaningful experience which
the child represents to her. This occurs in a dialogue
exchange between the two characters in which it is

apparent that in his own egocentricity the man cannot grasp the importance of the decision he is forcing upon the woman.

> "And we could have all this," she said. "And we could have everything and every day we make it more impossible."
> "What did you say?"
> "I said we could have everything."
> "We can have everything."
> "No, we can't."
> "We can have the world."
> "No, we can't."
> "We can go everywhere."
> "No, we can't. It isn't ours anymore."
> "It's ours."
> "No, it isn't. And once they take it away, you never get it back." (276)

The girl obviously realizes the wider implications of the proposed abortion. For her it has connotations beyond the simple physical act, and her choice of words in the responses augurs a spiritual and moral consequence. All of the dialogue exchanges between the two have an almost classic cast in the pathos of the divergence between them. The exchanges become an almost private *agon*, and at the symbolic level the outcome illustrates the theme of the story.

As the time of arrival of the train approaches, the central conflict resolves itself in an ambiguous fashion. The woman apparently realizes the absurdity of her efforts to translate her inner needs into terms which the man can understand. She makes her final plea in direct terms: " 'Would you please please please please please please please stop talking?' " And again, " 'I'll scream' " (277). It, too, goes unheard, and the man tries once again to rationalize his desire for the abortion. The tense pathos of the unsolved conflict is illustrated in the final exchange of the narrative: " 'Do you feel better?' he asked. 'I feel fine,' she said. 'There's nothing wrong with me. I feel fine' " (278). Her capitulation is a pathetic resolution, for throughout the story she is the one who has had insight.

In its totality the story portrays the sensibility of the woman thrust into conflict with the sterile life represented by the man. The pathos of her plight is ultimately sublimated into a pose of unconcern. But the repetition of the phrase "I feel fine" captures the emotional pitch of near-hysteria. The estrangement here takes the form of a clash of values, and it has as its basis a moral and spiritual framework. The man who cannot adjust to the processes of nature becomes the image of the alienated one who has divorced himself from the principle of life. He is a man who excuses moral sterility in the name of freedom, and, in spite of the literal outcome, the authorial tone indicates the unnatural consequence of such a position.

In "Cross-Country Snow" the central character, Nick, is pictured as a man who also feels trapped by the approaching birth of a child. In the story he is on a final skiing trip with a friend, George. When the two stop at an inn, their talk reveals Nick's inner feelings about the coming child. His attitudes are related in an exchange which concerns a pregnant, unfriendly waitress.

> "She isn't so cordial, is she?" said George.
> "Oh, well. She doesn't know us. . . . and then she's got that baby coming without being married and she's touchy."
> "How do you know she isn't married?"
> "No ring. Hell, no girls get married around here till they're knocked up." (186)

Nick's deprecating remark indicates his own feelings more than external fact, and his personal situation reveals the reason. His wife is to have a baby, and he must return to the United States. George acts as the register in the dialogue exchange when Nick directly articulates his unhappiness.

> "Is Helen going to have a baby?" George said, coming down to the table from the wall.
> "Yes."
> "When?"
> "Late next summer."
> "Are you glad?"
> "Yes. Now."
> "Will you go back to the States?"
> "I guess so."
> "Do you want to?"
> "No." (187)

The advent of parenthood means for Nick a severance from the irresponsibilities which Europe has offered. Although he is obviously unhappy, he has accepted this fact. To this degree he differs from the man in

"Hills Like White Elephants" who refuses to even consider acceptance of parenthood and loss of freedom.

Individuals may be ensnared in a number of ways, and they may have different degrees of insight into their plight. Love relationships that have gone awry provide a method of depicting individual responses to typically human involvements. Hemingway employs a number of different methods to illustrate the conflicts such ensnarements may cause to arise. In "A Canary for One," another story which treats the marriage theme, the entire meaning is suspended until the last line. What keeps this device from being mere gimmick, however, is that the accumulation of detail up to the ending in itself reveals a meaning which parallels the final resolution. The story is related by a first-person narrator. He tells of certain incidents which occur during a train ride to Paris. The purpose of this trip is withheld until the final line, and the whole narrative framework pivots at this point: "We were returning to Paris to set up separate residences" (342). To dramatize what the narrator-character feels about his personal situation, Hemingway not only withholds the information until the end but also introduces a meeting on the train with a middle-aged American woman who tells of the disruption of the love affair of her daughter. In so doing, she at the same time reveals her own insensibility to the love relationship. The canary she carries and takes care of becomes the symbol of love fettered and cared for in an artificial fashion by the same force which ultimately destroys its spirit.

The narrator's concern for minute details during the trip, his close account of the woman and her story, and his apparent dispassionate attitude in light of the ultimate conclusion function in much the same manner as does Nick's attention to the details of fishing in "Big Two-Hearted River." The tediousness of the woman and her boorish unfeeling for her daughter's attempt to find love create a prolixity within the story itself, until the final revelation explains the narrator's attempt to sublimate his own intense feelings by fixing upon other, external details. The word "love" is a signification of the conflicting elements within the thematic content, and an exchange between the wife of the narrator and the American woman points out the irony of the term to those who are themselves estranged from love.

> "I know Vevey," said my wife. "We were there on our honeymoon."
> "Were you really? That must have been *lovely*. I had no idea, of course, that she'd fall in *love* with him."
> "It was a very *lovely* place," said my wife.
> "Yes," said the American lady. Isn't it *lovely?* Where did you stop there?" (341, italics added)

Hemingway uses details of setting which further heighten the tension within the narrative and foreshadow the final revelation. At one point the narrator notes: "We were passing three cars that had been in a wreck. They were splintered open and the roofs sagged in. 'Look,' I said. 'There's been a wreck'" (341). A little earlier in the narrative he had noted a farmhouse burning. It is obvious these details are direct referents for his own situation, but what they also imply is a value judgement on his part. Marital estrangement means a literal wrecking or burning of a relationship and a consequent ruin of the normal course of life. Love-relationships must be cared for in much the same fashion as a canary.

The "gimmick" ending to a sequence is only one of the many methods Hemingway employs to create the effects he desires within his fiction. In the marriage stories again and again he uses some dominant effect from which the whole of a story takes its meaning. In "The Sea Change" he portrays the adjustment of man to abnormality in the world and in himself by hinging the entire narrative upon a quotation from Alexander Pope. When one views the passage in its original form and context, its unusual occurrence in the story imposes an ironic cast which is almost imperceptible.

The story line of "The Sea Change" concerns a couple who are about to separate because the woman is going away with a Lesbian. At first the man is repulsed by the thought of such a relationship ("I'll kill her"), but his acquiescence at the conclusion signals his own capitulation and acceptance of vice: " 'Go on,' his voice sounded strange to him. . . . 'And when you come back tell me all about it.' His voice sounded very strange. He did not recognize it. She looked at him quickly. He was settled into something" (400). The change in attitude comes about after the woman has appealed to him on the grounds that he too has perverse tendencies.

"I'd like it better if you didn't use words like that [perversion]," the girl said. "There's no necessity to use a word like that."

"What do you want me to call it?"

"You don't have to call it. You don't have
to put any name to it."

"That's the name for it."

"No," she said. "We're made up of all sorts
of things. You've known that. You've used it
well enough."

"You don't have to say that again."

"Because that explains it to you."

"All right," he said. "All right." (400)

The appeal to the abnormal desires within him
and his recognition of that abnormality lead the
man into his decision. But at the same time he recognizes the change this self-illumination has worked:
"He was not the same-looking man as he had been
before he had told her to go" (400-01). The recognition in this instance is akin to acceptance. Hemingway contrasts the inner stress of the decision by
having the bartender give an objective account of
the man's appearance: " 'You look very well, sir,'
James said. 'You must have had a very good summer' " (401). The further irony is apparent. Presumably the liaison between the man and woman
developed and flourished during the summer months.
The fact that this relationship too has been unrecog-
nized vice and that his external appearance indicates
health, heightens the ironic perspective. In this light
the liaison between the woman and the Lesbian
reflects directly the man's own involvements.

The suggestive detail of the story gains range
and depth by Hemingway's subtle interjection of the
reference to Pope's *An Essay on Man*. During the

argumentative exchange, and just before the man accuses the woman of perversion, he tells her: " 'Vice is a monster of such fearful mien . . . that to be something or other needs but to be seen. Then we something, something, then embrace.' He could not remember the words. 'I can't quote,' he said" (399). The full quotation from Pope is as follows:

> Vice is a monster of so frightful mien,
> As, to be hated, needs but to be seen;
> Yet seen too oft, familiar with her face,
> We first endure, then pity, then embrace.[1]

The character's misquotation alters the sense of the passage, and by doing so it adds a sharp, ironic twist to the narrative. He recalls the verses as suggesting "we embrace," which would imply forgiveness of another's misdemeanor. But what actually happens in the story proper is exactly what is suggested in the passage by Pope. The man has already been exposed to vice so long that he finally embraces it. The irony of the implication here is obvious. The man has approached the problem from an original position of self-righteousness; what persuades him is not magnanimity, or some spiritual impulse, as much as the appeal to the abnormal within him. In fine, he has embraced vice, not the woman.

The opening lines of Epistle II of *An Essay on Man*, from which the quotation comes, read: "Know then thyself, presume not God to scan;/The proper study of mankind is man."[2] It cannot be certain how much Hemingway referred to Pope, but "The Sea Change" does reveal something important about the nature of man. Most of Hemingway's fiction conforms to Pope's dictum to study man, and Hemingway over and over grounds his materials in humanity. All of the marriage stories deal with human failings and attempt to focus upon the inner workings of man's dilemmas. Most of man's difficulties are based on his own failings, making him both victim and conspirator. The fact that man can be the victim and at the same time embrace the cause of his suffering in itself is the point at times; sometimes the revelation that such dilemmas exist in the world gives the stories function and purpose. Hemingway's focus upon the normal or upon the abnormal makes little difference, for the portrayal of individuals working out their separate destinies usually encompasses both.

In "Homage to Switzerland," the separation of man and wife becomes the metaphorical basis for the examination of the process of adjustment to emotional hurt. Hemingway incorporates a three-part division in the story as a device to give added dimension to the theme. Each part reflects some particular element of its own, and all three interact so as to illuminate each other. In each a similarity marks the settings, but the central situation varies enough to give the individual parts a separate identity.

In Part I, "Portrait of Mr. Wheeler in Montreaux," the train station setting which carries through to the other two parts is established. In the second and third, however, the locale changes from Montreaux to Vevey and to Territet. The surface situation in all three is identical: the Simplon-Orient Express is an hour late and the central character in each has a short time period in which to wait. What these characters do during this period reveals something of their own individual personalities, their inner conflicts, and their failures. The tripartite division provides three "portraits" of three separate individuals traveling on the same line, waiting for the same train, delayed the same amount of time, awaiting the train in the same kind of station, and surrounded by the same kinds of people. What differs in each is the individual response to the situation, and in this way Hemingway presents each individual as a sharpened image against the same setting.

In the first division, Mr. Wheeler's choice of activity during the interval illustrates his adolescent enjoyment of playing at sex. It also prepares the way for the more meaningful predicament of Mr. Johnson, the main character of the second part. While awaiting the train, Mr. Wheeler occupies himself with a "pressing" attack on the "virtue" of a waitress working in the station.

> "Fräulein," he called. The waitress came over.
> "What would you like, sir?"
> "You," he said.
> "You must not joke me like that."
> "I'm not joking."
> "Then you must not say it."
> "I haven't got time to argue," Mr. Wheeler said. "The train comes in forty minutes. If you'll go upstairs with me I'll give you a hundred francs." (423)

Wheeler is joking, however, and it is a rather perverse kind of joke at that. He knows that it is impossible for the waitress to consent, for there is really not enough time and there is no upstairs in the station. And, as the narrative indicates, he "did not care for women." The tempting of the waitress reflects a distorted conception of love, for the man does not wish any conclusion to his proposal. The fact that he can play safely, coupled with the narrative detail about his dislike of women, suggests that there is something abnormal in his sexual tendencies.

In Part II, "Mr. Johnson Talks about It at Vevey," a completely different concept of abnormality is examined. For Wheeler, in Part I, abnormality is a part of his individual psychology, and it probably represents an aberration; for Johnson, the abnormality rests in the fact that he has separated from the norm of the marriage state. During the interval that Johnson waits for the train, he attempts to divert his mind from thoughts of the emotional hurt by externalizing the inner difficulty into talk. His talk of the divorce to several train station porters does not prove to be effective, because the porters do not really sympathize with him. One, innocently enough, tags the plight of Johnson by characterizing his own feeling about marriage.

> "You like being married?" Johnson asked one of the porters.
> "What?"
> "You like the married state?"
> "Oui. C'est normale." (429)

Johnson agrees that it is the normal state, but as he indicates the choice in the matter was not his. At the conclusion, the central intelligence articulates the ineffectuality of his attempt to adjust in some way to the sense of loss: "Inside the cafe he had thought that talking about it would blunt it; but it had not blunted it; it had only made him feel nasty" (430).

The concluding portrait of the three parts, "The Son of a Fellow Member at Territet," relates an incident involving a rather cynical central character. He meets an old man who considers that membership in The National Geographic Society is of considerable importance. The focal point of the character's bitterness rests upon a continual play of ironic contrast. The old man considers everything associated with the Society to have importance, and the young central character tells him that his father was a member. When the old man suggests that he would like to meet the father some day, the apparent motive for the young man's cynicism emerges: " 'I'm sure he would have liked to meet you but he died last year. Shot himself, oddly enough' " (434). The expected emotional hurt of the young man contrasts sharply with his slighting comment. The reference to the incident as "odd" compresses and disguises the hurt in the mask of understatement. Coupled with the pitiable, misguided faith of the old man in the Society, a vivid irony is evident. Both individuals have misplaced their faith.

The three portraits of the main characters in this story reveal a moment in their lives when the mask is dropped and the essential personality shows through. The devices Hemingway uses to "freeze" his characters in time — the late train and the identical background — magnify the portraits considerably. These people become illustrative of a cross section of society on the journey of life. They are held up for a brief span of time so that the artist may place the glass upon them and examine their situation more closely. All artists do this, of course, but in this story the three-portrait form reveals a facet of the theme.

All of the marriage stories which deal with emotional crises, abnormality, alienation or isolation, or whatever other difficulty are part of the method Hemingway chose to illustrate man's efforts to somehow adjust to life's contingencies. The marriage metaphor is well suited to such an expression, since the husband-and-wife relationship represents the smallest unit wherein morality can operate. When something goes amiss at this level, the indication is that something more drastic is occurring in the wider areas of social intercourse. The alienation and isolation which characterize the individuals in these stories illustrate Hemingway's concern with the results of failure to achieve selfhood during the maturation process. For those who have never come to terms with the fundamental experiences of life before chronological maturation, unsatisfactory involvement in the expanded sphere of marriage presages catastrophe. These people face impossible tasks, for they are not capable of dealing with the greater demands of moral action.

Hemingway focuses upon marriage as a device

by which some people hope to bridge the gap of individuation. As these stories amply demonstrate, the chasm cannot be spanned. Signs of defeat — aloneness, cowardice, sexual deviation — immediately signal the impossibility of avoiding the necessary trials of selfhood. The approach Hemingway uses is indirect, for he gives no positive indication that true harmony in human affairs is possible. Yet his condemnatory tone indicts those who because of their own shortcomings fail to express selfhood in the marriage relationship or in any other moral sphere.

Chapter VII

The Hemingway Hero

HEMINGWAY'S CLEAREST PRESENTATION of man's attempt to preserve an ideal is reflected in a group of stories called here, rather loosely, the Hemingway hero stories. Most of them examine the manifold difficulties encountered on the journey toward individuation, and a few examine the process in its totality. Here men face the ultimate test, or some symbolic reflection of that test, by trying to rise above the contingencies of life. Some of the stories point to a final, almost transcendental element in Hemingway's thought which at first glance seems at odds with his naturalistic technique.

In Hemingway's treatment of the ideals a man may hold, he forces consideration of the efficacy of the commitment to an ideal in a world where values have been prostituted to other gods, chiefly Mammon and unfaith. The man who commits himself to these false ideals is personified by Hemingway as "No-man." Those who adhere to the ideal of self-fulfillment are in the minority, and their very existence becomes intolerable to the majority who follow another course. The outcome of such a situation is always the same: persecution of those who hold the individual ideal. In most of Hemingway's stories he consistently champions the ideal of individuality. In those stories where other forces seem to emerge victorious, there is an underlying author sympathy which laments the fate of man in a world which can no longer accept a valid ideal.

The journey toward individuation in Western culture is best personified by the life of Christ, and Hemingway resorts to this motif in a number of ways. In "Today is Friday," Hemingway constructs a capsule drama saturated with ironic commentary about the Crucifixion. He does not resort to preciosity to mock the ideal represented by Christ, nor is his dramatization condemnatory of Christianity in any way. His attitude is clearly illustrated by the refrain repeated several times by one of the Roman soldiers who witnesses the Crucifixion: "He was pretty good in there today." The reiteration establishes a sustained tone of wonder, and it more effectively reveals the narrative purpose than any direct sentiment. The approach to the myth of Christ is one of a lament for the passing of a system of life which could foster such a hero. Other heroes many times reflect the model of Christ in their search for some mode of self-fulfillment in a world which has already indicated that for those who follow the ideal, crucifixion will be the end result.

In order to view more precisely the inner workings of Hemingway's portrayal of some of his "strong" hero-characters, a closer look at the implications of the Christ motif is appropriate. Carl G. Jung discusses some of the more important considerations, and a brief examination of these views brings Hemingway's application of the tradition into brighter focus.

For Jung the modern Christian man is a victim of a spiritual and moral isolation and disorientation. Man finds himself in a predicament because of his own shortcomings, and not the least of these is to be found in the area of his religion. Christianity provides Western man with a ready-made pattern to follow, and were it simply a matter of following the pattern no doubt all would be well. But there are many obstructions. One of the most significant of these, Jung suggests, is revealed in the fact that "the ideal has been turned by superficial and formalistically-minded believers into an external object of worship, and it is precisely this veneration for the object that prevents it from reaching down into the depths of the soul and transforming it into a wholeness in keeping with the ideal."[1]

At one level the life of Christ provides an outstanding historical meaning of personality, and the conflicts faced by Christ are not unlike those presented to contemporary man. Jung attributes the intense persecution of nascent Christianity to the fact that it was in direct antithesis to the prevailing political authority of the time: "there arose a direct opponent of the Caesarean madness that afflicted not only the emperor, but every Roman as well: *Civis Romanus sum.*"[2] The story of Christ's temptation in the wilderness exemplifies, psychologically, the power with which he came into collision: "it was the power-intoxicated devil of the prevailing Caesarean psychology."[3] The devil personifies the objective psyche that held all of the people of the Roman Empire in its grip. The offer to Christ of all the kingdoms of the earth was an attempt to make an earthly Caesar of him.

As an archetype of the hero, the one who is to achieve "wholeness," Christ recognized the nature of the objective psyche which had taken over the men of his times. For this reason, Jung argues, Christ did not attempt to suppress the manifestation of such psychic contents. Christ, by His crucifixion, represents a conscious assimilation of the Caesarean projections. In Jungian terms assimilation amounts to overcoming, and the story of Christ illustrates this victory.

Apart from any religious connection, and viewing the historical Christ solely as a hero figure, Jung explains the tremendous elevation of Christ as hero: "This apparently unique life became a sacred symbol because it is the psychological prototype of the only meaningful life, that is, of a life that strives for the individual realization — absolute and unconditional — of its own particular law."[4] It is just such a portrait that Hemingway paints of the very strong heroes in his fiction, and all of the central characters may be measured against the test of self-fulfillment.

The figure of Christ crucified for the sins of mankind as a central character in any dramatization might force the subject matter to the level of sentimentality. Such an element would be ludicrous in relation to the situational connotations and the magnitude of the Crucifixion theme. Hemingway rarely falls into such a trap, no matter what the subject matter. In "Today is Friday" he avoids all such pitfalls by approaching his subject obliquely. The three

soldiers who were present at the Crucifixion occupy
the center of the stage, but the focus is elsewhere.
The drama is hardly more than a vignette, and its
length, coupled with the wine-shop setting and the
colloquialisms of the dialogue, forces a cataclysmic
event into an almost absurd compression. Yet the
effect of the employment of these stylistic devices is
such that, working on the correlative cultural con-
ditioning of his audience, Hemingway achieves a
subtlety of emotional response and evokes a tremendous reader sympathy for his subject.

The title of the piece implies an authorial comment upon the complicity of contemporary man in
the events described within the drama. The casting
of the dialogue into "tough-guy," soldier jargon
("Hey, what you put in that, camel chips?" [356])
translates the episode into a modern idiom. Hemingway also gains his purpose through characterization,
since the soldiers as well as the Hebrew wine-seller
are all disinterested persons. In this way the dramatic
perspective suggests an objective treatment of the
subject matter. Still, two of the characters, the "1st
Roman Soldier" and the "3d Roman Soldier," reveal
their sympathy with Christ's actions on the cross.

The admiration of the two Roman soldiers contrasts with the skepticism of the "2d Roman Soldier":
" 'You guys don't know what I'm talking about. I'm
not saying whether he was good or not. What I mean
is, when the time comes. When they first start nailing
him, there isn't none of them wouldn't stop if they
could' " (357). One further contrast is illustrated by
George, the Hebrew wine-seller and prototype of the

disinterested bartender: " 'No, I didn't take any interest in it, Lootenant' " (357).

The obvious view of Christ taken by the characters within the drama is that He was human. This device serves Hemingway's ends. In a reflex of the surface irony, an underlying level of muted irony reveals the author's tone and sheds light on the stories patterned after the motif of the *imitatio Christi*. The fact that Christ's performance on the cross has aroused sympathy on the part of the two soldiers suggests the possibility that Christ is a pertinent symbol for society in His role as the redeeming hero. The reference is slight, but it is supported in the drama by the illness of one of the soldiers. The suggestion is that the event he has witnessed has disturbed him more deeply than he can say. " 'I got a gut-ache,' " he tells his companions. This statement reflects the nausea of other Hemingway characters who become ill after witnessing events that probe to the core of their emotional responses.

The direct treatment of the Crucifixion as a theme in "Today is Friday" gathers importance in its relation to the themes of many of Hemingway's other short stories. In particular it provides a parallel for those which treat a central character who holds an ideal not compatible with that of his world. Jung's comment concerning Christ's conscious assimilation of the Caesarean tendencies of his time is appropriate in other terms to Hemingway's depiction of a hero figure in "The Undefeated." Not that the conflict in that story specifically involves a contest between a hero and the forces of the "power-intoxicated devil," but the contest is a parallel with Christ's struggle, and the two are not totally unlike. Hemingway couches the struggle in terms of a ritualistic engagement between man and bull, and this suggests a conflict of forces beyond mere literal notation.

Much has been written about the importance of the bullfight in Hemingway's fiction, and most of it is appropriate. An examination of Hemingway's direct declaration on the subject and a comparison with the implications of such stories as "Today is Friday" reveal that its centrality in Hemingway's thought goes far beyond the obvious. When seen as part of a general concept of a pastoral type of hero who is again and again crucified because of his ideals, such expressions reveal clearly that there is operative in Hemingway's fiction an ideal which at one level, at least, merges with the traditional Christian notion of crucifixion and redemption.

In many ways, already partly touched upon in the introduction to this study, Hemingway's non-fictional account of bullfighting, *Death in the Afternoon*, provides a touchstone for an understanding of the premises upon which much of the fiction rests. It soon becomes obvious in that work that the bullfight suggests a meaningful ritual activity for Hemingway, and his explanations point to his precise feelings on the subject. In spite of the many metaphorical allusions to bullfighting, his direct, contextual employment of the bullfight is to be found chiefly in one novel, *The Sun Also Rises*, and in two short stories, "The Undefeated" and "The Capital of the World." It otherwise appears in six of the "interchapters" of *In Our Time*, as well as in a number of nonfiction accounts.

Hemingway describes the bullfight as an "art." As such, it is capable of providing an aesthetic experience. Its nature is tragic: "The bullfight is not a sport in the Anglo-Saxon sense of the word, that is, it is not an equal contest or an attempt at an equal contest between a bull and a man. Rather it is a tragedy; the death of the bull, which is played, more or less well, by the bull and the man involved and in which there is danger for the man but certain death for the animal."[5] The tragic nature of bullfighting is controlled by a rigidly disciplined ritual, and this has a threefold division, *los tres tercios de la lidia*, or the three thirds of combat.

Hemingway suggests that these "thirds" are analogous to the three acts in tragedy. The first, the *suerte de varas*, or trial of the lances, is the "act" of the capes, the picadores and the horses, and in it "the bull has the greatest opportunity to display his bravery or cowardice."[6] The second "act" includes the planting of the *banderillos* in the bull's neck, "so that his attack will be slower, but surer and better directed."[7] In the final "act" the matador prepares the bull for killing. Hemingway's own summary is necessary here for its bearing on the nuances of meaning he associates with the bullfight.

> These are the three acts in the tragedy of the bullfight, and it is the first one, the horse part, which indicates what the others will be and, in fact, makes the rest possible. It is in the first act that the bull comes out in full possession of all his faculties, confident, fast, vicious and conquering. All his victories are in the first act. At the end of the first act he has apparently won.

Three acts in /fishing

He has cleared the ring of mounted men and is alone. In the second act he is baffled completely by an unarmed man and very cruelly punished by the banderillos so that his confidence and his blind general rage goes and he concentrates his hatred on an individual object. In the third act he is faced by only one man who must, alone, dominate him by a piece of cloth placed over a stick, and kill him from in front, going in over the bull's right horn to kill him with a sword thrust between the arch of his shoulder blades.[8]

For Hemingway the bullfight carries the further possibility of some sort of aesthetic-cathartic response, and he directly articulates this: "I feel very fine while it is going on and have a feeling of life and death and immortality, and after it is over I feel very sad but very fine."[9] All men do not have this capacity, of course, and in relation to those who view the bullfight it belongs only to a select few: "The aficionado, or lover of the bullfight, may be said, broadly, then, to be one who has this sense of tragedy and ritual of the fight."[10]

With the ritual of the bullfight as the meaningful base, Hemingway actually constructs a hierarchy by which, in this special sense, the morality of an individual may be measured. It is not too distant from the gauge of the hero as he appears in the short stories in his quest for individuation. The "high priest" in this instance would be the matador himself, but only if he performs the functions of his office correctly and is the "complete bullfighter." The aficionado comes next, for he is the one who has the tragic sense and vicariously participates in the ritual at which the matador officiates. At the lowest end of the scale are those people who attend the bullfight and view the ritual performance but do not understand. These mere onlookers are the "tourists," the "well-fed, skull and bones-ed, porcellian-ed, beach-tanned, flannelled, panama-hatted, sport-shod ones."[11]

The distinction among the levels of the hierarchy is related to the rest of the Hemingway canon, for an obvious value judgement based on an ideal is implied. Being a "complete bullfighter," the object of the ideal, may seem trivial at first glance, but when taken as a metaphor for a dominant attitude that persists through most of Hemingway's work, its importance gains magnitude. The appearance of an ideal other than stoicism has implications in relation to the traditional views of Hemingway's art. That is, idealism is not a framework in which Hemingway has often been thought to work.

Another important aspect of the bullfight as ritual concerns Hemingway's edict that as an art it deals with death. For Hemingway violent death is one of the simple and fundamental elements of life. Out of this view he derives a basic attitude that appears in many forms in his fiction: the only certainty in life is death. Atonement, with death as a certainty, formulates the ultimate task of many Hemingway heroes, and the motif in itself is a universal pattern. In the bullfight, as in other methods of seeking atonement, all efforts of the hero are directed toward reconciliation with the knowledge of death. Whether or not the rituals are effective is always determined more by the individual attributes of the hero than by external circumstance. Regardless of the particular situation, the Hemingway hero is always concerned with the problem of death. If he can become the equivalent of the "complete bullfighter," the possibility of atonement or eventual transcendence to some greater level of self-realization is ever-present. The type of hero that can accomplish such a feat is rare in any area of life, and the small likelihood of his ever appearing is related by Hemingway in connection with his discussion of the appearance of the "complete bullfighter": "But waiting for a messiah is a long business and you get many fake ones. There is no record in the Bible of the number of fake messiahs that came before Our Lord, but the history of the last ten years of bullfighting would record little else."[12]

The recognition that death is inevitable is only one part of the ritual, for the *way* one faces death has equal importance. For Hemingway it is here that man records his true dignity or cowardice. The whole of the matter is not, however, simply that one understands that death will come and that he must prepare for it. On the contrary, the adjustment to death becomes a complex ritual in itself.

At the close of *Death in the Afternoon*, Hemingway relates that he took no formal notice of the "young phenomena" in the bullfight of the time. The reason for this inattention, he says, is that one cannot adequately judge a bullfighter until he has received his first serious wound. Similarly, in the fiction a hero can only prove his merit after he has been "wounded" in some fashion by the experiences of life. In much of Hemingway's fiction the wound is depicted as some physical hurt which either represents some deep inner hurt or foreshadows an emotional hurt. Accordingly the wound itself becomes just as much a certainty as death; indeed, the two are inextricably bound together. An identical situation exists in the bullfight, as Hemingway sees it, for it is a foregone conclusion that the matador will be gored if he continues to fight. The stroke is simply a matter of time, as is the case in the life experience, and the length of time depends upon the skill of the individual in avoiding the horns — either literally or metaphorically. Once a bullfighter has received a horn wound, if he lives and makes the proper adjustment he will be a better bullfighter and will approach the ideal. If he does not adjust to the certainty of the wound and to eventual death, he becomes a coward and does not truly participate in the ritual.

The "complete bullfighter" makes such an infrequent appearance in Hemingway's fiction that it is difficult to discern his attributes. Pedro Romero in *The Sun Also Rises* is often thought to represent the ideal of a pure and uncontaminated individual; however he represents more of the possibility of the ideal than the ideal itself. Although he faces the bull in an exemplary manner after having been "wounded" by Cohn's fists, he is still young and would have to repeat such experiences over and over to be adequately judged. In other novels and stories the individual who has met the experiences of life and death and has in some way adjusted to them appears sometimes as a shadow figure and sometimes in broad relief. These characters are the old, learned ones who figure many times in the capacity of an almost magic-guide personage. Sometimes too a mock-guide figure appears and attempts to lead the hero away from the meaningful experience. At any event, the adjusted one is not always the representative of the ideal, for his adjustment may indicate a compromise which the true idealist would not be willing to make.

In "The Capital of the World" Hemingway illustrates the extreme dangers for the man who would become the "complete bullfighter" and follow the ideal. The juxtaposition of the boy facing the knives of the mock-bull while the cowardly bullfighter makes advances to his sister provides a contrast and marks the differences between the two modes of adjustment. The boy as the uninitiated one exhibits characteristics that might have made him a "complete bullfighter," if he had lived. His early death signifies the almost impossible task that faces the man who would pursue the ideal.

"The Undefeated" examines a further facet of man's striving to maintain his grasp of the ideal. The central character's refusal to accept the inevitable passing away of every man in many ways captures the essence of Hemingway's views of the process of individuation. In this story the fusion of the concept of the "complete bullfighter" with the parallel Christian ideal comes about. The bullfighter, Manuel Garcia, has grown too old to fight effectively; he is reduced to fighting in the "Nocturnals." His refusal to accept this fact precipitates the climactic wound he receives in the story. His very refusal, however, is what gives him stature, for it points to the parallel theme of crucifixion on the cross of an ideal.

The bullfight as subject matter for fiction allows Hemingway to symbolize the totality of the life and death principle. In it are contained the archetypal constructs inherent in every redemptive religious mystery that man has ever devised. Utilizing its contents as a fictional device in "The Undefeated," Hemingway implicitly points to the possibility of an individual undergoing the redemptive ordeal of suffering. The very refusal of the central character to quit in spite of the certain consequence of wound and death places him in the context of the perennial hero — the Christ who must be sacrificed over and over in the celebration of the mass in order to renew the spirituality of all mankind.

The fact that Manuel must undergo this redemptive ordeal at night is at once suggestive at two levels. At the literal level he is forced to fight in the "Nocturnals" because these are the lesser fights. They include the "Charlie Chaplin's" and utilize bulls that "the veterinaries won't pass in the daytime" (237). Symbolically, the "Nocturnals" relate to the basis of the ultimate conflict: Manuel must face the unknown and confront the representative of the irrational forces of darkness. In a traditional way the story is set in darkness: the night-voyage, the precondition of the journey into selfhood. Cast into this mold, the form of the story contributes to the symbolism of the redeeming hero.

The relationship between Manuel and Zurito, the old knowing picador, condenses the implications of the theme into a symbolic portrait of the traditional father-son relationship. Zurito is the strong figure, the authority-guide, to whom Manuel must go for aid in the coming fight. As a retired picador who has performed his trade well, Zurito is the personification of the "adjusted one," the man who has faced the bulls over and over and who has accepted the coming of age and the loss of vigor. The exchange which follows Zurito's reluctant consent to pic for Manuel illustrates the authority versus "innocent" relationship.

> "You ought to quit it, Manolo."
>
> "I can't," Manuel said. "I'm going good now, I tell you."
>
> Zurito leaned forward, his hands on the table.
>
> "Listen, I'll pic for you and if you don't go big tomorrow night, you'll quit. See? Will you do that?"
>
> "Sure."
>
> Zurito leaned back, relieved.
>
> "You got to quit," he said. "No monkey business. You got to cut the coleta." (244)

In the context of the authority-innocent complex, Zurito plays the role of the wise old man. Manuel, chronologically only ten years his junior, continues his commitment to the ideal and thus is cast in the role of the young, uninitiated one. But Manuel has been initiated, and it is this which elevates him to the greater role. Zurito, although the wiser in the ways of the world, and although he has been a great picador, cannot really compete with Manuel on the ground of idealism. His inability to comprehend Manuel's motivations reveal that his "adjustment" is in one sense a compromise of the ideal. That is, one must act this way if he is to sur-

vive in the world. Yet this conduct may not be the
"best" way from the moral and spiritual standpoint.
Manuel refuses to make such a compromise. Thus
the ideal remains uncorrupted and Manuel rises in
stature.

Whenever a figure such as Zurito appears in
Hemingway's fiction, the case is similar. He has
"adjusted," but adjustment is partial surrender. For
this reason the guide-authority figure — father or wise
old man — can help the hero in his quest up to a
certain point; thereafter, success or failure rests
solely with the individual. Zurito can advise Manuel
and pic the bull in such a way that Manuel can
properly handle him, but in the final analysis all
authority must come from within when Manuel faces
the bull: "He had not seen Zurito. Where was Zurito?"
(262). So it is that, when that much abused "moment
of truth" arrives, the wounded Manuel himself re-
affirms the transcendent possibilities of all mankind:
"All right, you bastard! Manuel drew the sword
out of the muleta, sighted with the same movement,
and flung himself onto the bull. He felt the sword
go in all the way. Right up to the guard. Four fingers
and his thumb into the bull. The blood was hot on
his knuckles, and he was on top of the bull" (264).

Manuel has achieved victory over something
greater than a mere bull, and Hemingway indicates
the wider meaning in the description of Manuel's
thoughts and views immediately after the kill: "He
was sitting down looking at something. It was the
bull. His four feet up. Thick tongue out. Things
crawling around on his belly and under his legs.
Crawling where the hair was thin. Dead bull. To

hell with the bull! To hell with them all!" (264). The sordid details suggest that Manuel has overcome the representative of all the forces which have blocked his bid for complete mastery of himself, and his condemnation of both bull and society represents the fierce individuality which his victory has brought to the surface.

The victory over the forces of compromise is pointed up by the reference to the bull's testicles. With Manuel's defeat of the bull, almost totemistically he assimilates the vitality of the animal. Zurito's decision not to cut Manuel's coleta—a phallic symbol —reflects his acknowledgment of the victory he has witnessed, in spite of the wound Manuel has received. The point is, of course, that the wound is of no consequence in light of the emergence of Manuel's true character. As the father-authority figure, Zurito has witnessed, symbolically, the "crucifixion" of the son in defense of the ideal. This leaves the "adjusted" Zurito somewhat abashed, as the narrative reveals: "The doctor's assistant put the cone over Manuel's face and he inhaled deeply. Zurito stood awkwardly, watching" (266).

The pattern of ritual in "The Undefeated" clearly approximates the motif of crucifixion and redemption in the Christ story. In this instance the bullfight serves as the symbolic frame upon which Hemingway projects his theme. Manuel emerges as the personification of the "complete" bullfighter, for his refusal to submit to defeat on any grounds illustrates the same principle that Christ did: both are the "undefeated."

Defeat signifies surrender of the ideal, and the

true hero in Hemingway's terms is the individual who never accepts the compromise. The end is always the same, however, for the world which Hemingway describes cannot tolerate the true individual for long. The victory for a hero is essentially the overcoming of the sordidness of the world in which he lives, and the knowledge such a success brings makes him unsuitable to live in that world. In another story, "The Short Happy Life of Francis Macomber," a like pattern evolves. The victory of Macomber over himself releases him, but at the same time it condemns him to death.

Hemingway centers the surface conflicts around the traditional coming-of-age story. The participants are Macomber, his wife, and Wilson, a white hunter. The story line concerns a hunting safari in Africa. During this excursion the infidelity of Macomber's wife is brought to the surface by Macomber's demonstration of cowardice. Her affair is with Wilson, who symbolizes for her the personification of the traits which her own husband lacks. When Macomber finally achieves his manhood by demonstrating his courage, his wife recognizes the change as an omen of her own demise and "accidentally" shoots him. The whole story pivots on the ironic circumstances of a man who dies just at the moment when he has learned to live — thus, the "short happy life." Macomber's coming-of-age is an irony in itself, since he has already reached a chronological age where maturity should have been reached. The fact that he learns in Africa, the wilderness, suggests a further level of interpretation.

The three characters in the story posit a triangular conflict beyond the secondary love-triangle which functions only as the catalyst for Macomber's trial of learning. What each figure represents is an impulse within the construct of the nursery drama. The jungle setting, in fact, suggests the same sort of wilderness that appears as the setting of "Indian Camp" and the other learning stories that treat a young hero. The guide through this wilderness is Wilson. In his capacity of literal guide, and in his somewhat cynical and detached attitude, he is not unlike an authority-father figure. The wife performs the office of the dangerous mother-temptress who holds the innocent in bondage. Macomber's final breaking of the maternal bond by performing the function of the father figure — hunting well and being brave — explains at the psychological level the necessity for the mother-wife to kill him.

One would not want to make too much of the analogy, but Hemingway himself couches the drama in sexual terms. Morality takes its meaning in the story by the measure of sexual fidelity. Macomber has never been a man true to himself, and his wife's infidelity mirrors this inner state. Although the wife has been unfaithful in the past, the central situation of the story objectifies the infidelity-cowardice theme: Macomber's fear precipitates the wife's affair with Wilson. The parallel is brought directly into focus when Macomber's wife returns from Wilson's tent.

"Where have you been?" Macomber asked in the darkness.

"Hello," she said. "Are you awake?"

"Where have you been?"

"I just went out to get a breath of air."

"You did, like hell."

"What do you want me to say, darling?"

"Where have you been?"

"Out to get a breath of air."

"That's a new name for it. You *are* a bitch."

"Well, you're a coward."

"All right," he said. "What of it?" (22)

When Macomber can express moral outrage, he has taken a first step toward manhood. Hemingway has already interjected a detail which foreshadows such a step, and, in fact, it is part of the controlling symbol of the story. While Macomber's wife has been with Wilson, Macomber has been reliving the whole experience of his flight of cowardice from the lion. And, too, just before the wife returns to the tent, Macomber has a dream which signals his coming change of character: "It was now about three o'clock in the morning and Francis Macomber, who had been asleep a little while after he had stopped thinking about the lion, wakened and then slept again, woke suddenly, frightened in a dream of the bloody-headed lion standing over him" (22). The lion becomes in this sequence the manifestation of Macomber's cowardice, and its appearance in the dream represents the force which must be overcome.

The lion becomes the totemistic symbol of both the father-authority, the lover of the mother-wife, and the symbol of the new self which Macomber must become in order to usurp the father's couch. The appearance of the bloody head further suggests the guilt feelings such an ordeal necessarily arouses.

Wilson is the human personification of the traits which the lion incorporates, and always he is described with reference to the color red — a symbol of passion and vitality. For example, Mrs. Macomber refers to him as "the beautiful red-faced Mr. Robert Wilson" (21); and Macomber says to his wife at one point: " 'I hate that red-faced swine' " (25). The narrative description also refers to Wilson many times by use of the color: "He was about middle height with sandy hair, a stubby mustache, a very red face and extremely cold blue eyes" (4). When Mrs. Macomber holds her husband in contempt and looks to Wilson as the husband-surrogate, Hemingway marks the attachment with further color symbolism by associating Mrs. Macomber with a near-color of red: "the rose-colored, sun-proofed shirt she wore" (5), or "looking pretty rather than beautiful in her faintly rosy khaki" (10). When Macomber later gains his courage, a fact which his wife cannot reconcile, she is described several times over as "white-faced." By use of the color device, Hemingway thus paints in thin outline the passing of courage and vitality — the blood of the lion — from Wilson and Mrs. Macomber to Macomber.

Having associated Wilson with the lion, and having coalesced the two into a symbol of the new self which Macomber is to become, Hemingway climaxes the sequence with the dream of the bloody lion's head. From this point on in the narrative Macomber gains stature by carefully defined stages. Although he has put up with his wife's infidelity for years, immediately after the dream he becomes outraged over her actions. Next he begins to hate Wilson, a mark of inner courage since Wilson has been to this point a guide-figure: "You bastard, thought Macomber, you insolent bastard" (23). His moral outrage proves to be the outward token of his inner change, and he is "disgusted" with his wife and Wilson — a fact which resembles the nausea of other characters in Hemingway. The final encounter with the buffalo illustrates overtly the inner change of character: " 'You know, I'd like to try another lion,' Macomber said. 'I'm really not afraid of them now. After all, what can they do to you?' " (32).

In terms of the psychology of the drama, once Macomber has reached this position the assertion is equivalent to the deed; Macomber has achieved his manhood. Having done so, he has severed the maternal-wife bond and achieved freedom from domination. The final shooting is anti-climactic, for it represents the woman's inability to recognize the freedom of the husband-son figure. As far as Macomber's character is concerned, however, he has achieved atonement with the father as authority figure — he can do and feel as Wilson can. He has, in terms of the symbolism, become the lion. Wilson realizes this alteration fully, and he explains it to the woman in terms of a mother and son separation: "He *would* have left you too" (36).

The full cycle of the journey toward individuation depicted in "The Short Happy Life of Francis Macomber" illustrates in much the same fashion as "The Undefeated" the inevitable results of such a victory in an ideal-less world. And Macomber's death is a direct result of his having approached the ideal. Wilson, on the other hand, can continue to live because he has "adjusted." Hemingway points this out in the narrative in a direct manner. Wilson has only one ideal, and that is in the area of hunting. Thus he is limited in the moral sense, for in other areas he accepts the "standards" of those with whom he associates: "Their standards were his standards as long as they were hiring him" (26). Macomber, having learned by way of Wilson's one moral province, indicates he will carry the ideal over into other areas of moral action. This commitment proves unacceptable, for the world will have none of it. Macomber's point of conflict with the world apart from his own inner sphere is the marital relationship. Having been true to himself — the reverse of the position he held earlier in the moral equation — he rejects his wife's infidelity — the constant in the equation — and at the same time courts death.

The great danger of succumbing to the lures of the world, of "adjusting" as Wilson has done, is illustrated again in "The Snows of Kilimanjaro." If a man gives in at one point, the temptation to give in at all points is ever present. A capitulation of this nature is what has happened to Harry, the central character of "The Snows of Kilimanjaro." The form of the story is that of the traditional lament for a lost life. In its approach the story is not dissimilar to the Old English "Deor," "Wanderer," and "The Wife's Lament." That is, it is part of the tradition in literature of the lament for the passing of life and for missed opportunities. From the authorial perspective and because of the author's personal situation at the time of writing,[13] the story may be a kind of prose elegy, following that traditional form.

Whatever the tradition, the form of the story conveys the tale of a dying man lamenting a misused life. It is this fictional structure which points to the theme of individuation.

The story fits into the pattern of stories which involve an intense focus upon a single, central character, and it examines by subjective response the events of a past life as this character reviews them. A more important theme in relation to the individual emerges here, for the thematic vehicle rests upon a question: What is the nature of death? As it turns out, death comes in many guises, and the symbols which depict it are a catalogue of the central character's life: buzzard, hyena, women, and money. The final approach to death, however, relates to none of these, for it comes in the form of "Old Compie," the pilot who "saves" Harry at the end of the story. It is Harry's ascendence into death in an almost ironic fashion upon which the entire theme of the story hinges.

Each of the death symbols reflects some role Harry has played in his life or represents some attachment which has led him into a life of sterility. The pilot of the long awaited plane functions somewhat differently, for he appears in the dream sequence at the end and carries Harry off toward Kilimanjaro: "And then he knew that there was where he was going" (76). Kilimanjaro is identified in the epigraph appended to the story as: "the Masai 'Ngàje Ngài,' the House of God" (52). The transporting of Harry to Kilimanjaro reveals that Compie is the final guide who will lead him, at least within the logic of his own inner drama, to a kind of redemptive Avalon now that he has recognized all his failings.

As Harry approaches each stage of self-realization, the death symbols enter as a kind of mockery of his past and underline his development. His whole purpose in journeying to Africa to achieve some sort of renewal is stated directly in the narrative: "Africa was where he had been happiest in the good time of his life, so he had come out here to start again" (59). The buzzards and the hyena function as the two natural symbols of death. The fact that they are scavengers parallels Harry's self-accusation that he has betrayed his real self for women and money. Both women and money are symbols of the social and material evils which have effectively killed Harry's art: "But, in yourself, you said that you would write about these people; about the very rich; that you were really not of them but a spy in their country; that you would leave it and write of it and for once it would be written by some one who knew what he was writing of" (59). Harry has not only violated his art but also pandered his sexual vitality to achieve security. At one point he tells his wife, cynically, " 'Love is a dunghill . . . and I'm the cock that gets on it to crow' " (57). In his recall of past experiences, Harry recognizes he has lost the chance to live an effective life true to himself.

Death finally comes to Harry in an unexpected way. Throughout, he watches the figures of the birds and the hyena in anticipation that they are the harbingers of death. At times he even reflects upon the many guises of death and the way it will finally arrive: "He lay still and death was not there. It must have gone around another street. It went in pairs, on bicycles, and moved absolutely silently on the pavements" (71). Yet the irony of the mode in which death arrives evolves into a resolution of the question posed throughout. Death may be a form of transcendence if the subject has undergone an ordeal of suffering and if he has achieved insight and illumination. The plight which Harry laments is symptomatic of the same "disease" which afflicts all of the Hemingway heroes in the short stories who would strive for the ideal. Having missed the ideal throughout his life, Harry recaptures the view of his youthful strivings. Death, therefore, is anti-climactic.

Although couched in bitter and naturalistic terms, the lament of Harry is nonetheless a tragic one which posits an ideal of truth. Harry's situation at the literal level is a pathetic one, to be sure, but his mental journey, his recapitulation of his misspent life, purges him of his errant ways. Compie's entrance at the conclusion of the narrative indicates that a transformative process has taken place. Had the situation remained in the realm of the literal, death might have been depicted by the hyena symbol. As it turns out, the appearance of the hyena is more of a comment on the world Harry has left than on Harry himself. Harry is thus more properly identified with the leopard mentioned in the epigraph which was seeking the summit.

Pandering to the representative forces of materialism and its various offspring too long, or having been exposed to life's contingencies and having "adjusted" to them, may suddenly force the individual into a situation where he must "take up his cross," as it were, and suffer the fate of those who live directly the life that leads to crucifixion. In fact the adjusted state may itself become a kind of ideal, although it is never the purest in Hemingway's hierarchy. The figure who appears in the stories as "the one who knows," a Zurito or a Wilson, may have had to make compromises en route in order to stay alive in the world, but he still has that degree of strength and self-knowledge which fits him for the task of the ideal when he is forced. Hemingway to some degree seems to excuse the deviation from the ideal on the grounds of survival, for it is obvious in such stories as "Today is Friday," "The Undefeated," and "The Capital of the World" that total commitment leads to death.

In "Fifty Grand," Hemingway presents the portrait of an individual who exemplifies the thesis of the "adjusted" one. The character in this case is a boxer, Jack, who holds the championship. Knowing he is too old to win against a younger opponent, he bets against himself. The irony evolving out of this situation concerns the fact that the gamblers with whom he has placed his bet attempt to betray him. The result is that he must — at a late stage of his career and in spite of his motive — undergo a severe test of his courage, and this ordeal finally transcends the immoral quality of his wager. In effect he is a Faustus trying to foil a Mephistopheles who is a symbolization of his own inner tendencies.

The real irony pervading this story of a final trial by ordeal is that the act of courage belies the central character's view of himself and his role. As the old, experienced one, Jack sees in fighting no significance beyond that of an occupation. His view is sharpened by contrast with the more naïve and innocent view of Jerry, the "I" of the story. As a character, the narrator performs the function of a register against which the views of the fighter are contrasted. The juxtaposition of the two attitudes effects a conflict of values. At one point, for example, when the two are discussing the bet the exchange clearly defines each attitude.

> "Fifty grand is a lot of money," I said.
> "It's business," said Jack. "I can't win. You know I can't win anyway."
> "As long as you're in there you got a chance."
> "No," Jack says. "I'm all through. It's just business." (315)

In spite of what Jack maintains, his endurance and courage—the result of a low blow from his opponent —cast his actions into a meaningful *agon*. The contest he has entered is beyond the physical realm; it involves a conflict with the forces of immorality. The ironic victory is the loss of the fight in spite of the betrayal. And his method of winning — delivering a low blow of his own — suggests that his "adjustment" has limits, and he defeats the forces of immorality upon their own grounds.

Another story, "After the Storm," centers upon a character with similar attributes. Although neither Jack in "Fifty Grand" nor the "I" of "After the Storm" yields to the rule of conventional morality, they both illustrate man's victory over himself and adjustment to the world in which he lives. The "I" of the latter story participates in what amounts to an *agon* of immoral illegality. Yet he is the hardened one who, accustomed to life's contingencies, does not blush at its sordidness. In terms of his own ethic, his actions are moral, much the same as are those of Jack in his ethical sphere.

The central character of "After the Storm" has adjusted to the extreme challenges of his environment. The opening scene portrays him in a barroom fight and prepares the way for the flight to sea: "He was choking me and hammering my head on the floor and I got the knife out and opened it up; and I cut the muscle right across his arm and he let go of me" (372). In his flight from the legal consequences of his actions in the barroom, the "I" goes out in his boat and just off shore discovers a liner sunk by a storm. He tries over and over to reach the liner and enter it in order to loot. After experiencing a nose-bleed and considerable physical hardship, he leaves. A new storm keeps him away for a week, and when he returns he finds the liner empty: "Well, the Greeks got it all. Everything. They must have come fast all right. They picked her clean. First there was the birds, then me, then the Greeks, and even the birds got more out of her than I did" (378). This final comment illustrates the point of the story. The environment is jungle-like in its fierce competition, and the spoils of the misfortune of others belong to those who are capable of getting what they can. In this case the "I" does not get anything, but that is of no consequence in relation to the focus of the story.

The piece, illustrative of the adjustment process, approaches the subject obliquely. It is more an attitudinal examination than a dramatized sequence of action. The "I" exhibits his adjustment by his viewpoint. He accepts rather objectively the idea that the spoils have been taken before he can conquer the hazards of the venture. He also equates himself with the other scavengers — the birds and the Greeks — who live from the stricken. Such an acceptance illustrates his knowledge of the ways of the environment. The morality operative here is that of the jungle, and his attitude displays his forcefulness as a participant.

"The Gambler, The Nun, and The Radio" examines other adjustments people make to the exigencies of life. The central character of the story is Mr. Frazer. From the vantage point of a hospital room he reflects on the various responses, including his own, to the life situation. The courage of a wounded Mexican, Cayetana Ruiz, at first seems to illustrate the ideal, but as Frazer finds out it is only the Mexican's way of adjusting. Most of the traits of the Mexican are those of the true Hemingway hero, however, for above all he has self-knowledge. The very fact that he knows his own limitations has always allowed him to escape any serious consequences from his occupation. The wound he has received this time is only a chance happening: " 'The first time,' he said. 'That has only happened once' " (484). Even the Nun, whose ideal is to become a saint, has made certain "adjustments" to the world. In fact, the whole story in one sense catalogues the adjustments people make. If they do not adjust, they start, as Frazer terms it, "thinking." The adjustment comes in a number of guises, but its function is always the same.

Religion is the opium of the people. . . . Yes, and music is the opium of the people. . . . And

now economics is the opium of the people;
along with patriotism the opium of the people
in Italy and Germany. What about sexual intercourse; was that an opium of the people? . . .
But drink was a sovereign opium of the people,
oh, an excellent opium. Although some prefer
the radio. . . . Along with these went gambling.
. . . Ambition was another, an opium of the
people, along with belief in any new form of gov-
ernment. . . . What was it? Of course; bread was
the opium of the people. (485-86)

Frazer's reduction of every conceivable activity
to an "opium" — an obvious play on the Marxist
"opiate" — illustrates his own basic difficulty. He is
the unadjusted one, the victim of total unfaith. Although he views with cynicism the various modes of
escape, in the conclusion he makes a tentative truce
of a sort. He too has a mode of adjustment, although
he recognizes its limitations in much the same way
as the gambler: "he would have a little spot of the
giant killer and play the radio, you could play the
radio so that you could hardly hear it" (487).

The adjustment of the older, wiser ones is further depicted in the story "A Clean Well-Lighted
Place." There, darkness is symbolized as the fear of
the unknown, or the fear of death. When considered
as an adjustment to life, the characters' method seems
extreme and escapist; actually, what these characters
have adjusted to is death. In this instance, as the title
points out, the adjustment takes the form of an avoid-
ance. These men are not the ones who follow the way
to the ideal. Only the young waiter has "illusions,"
and his are not the best. The older waiter has acquired

an adjustment which parallels that of the old man around whom the story revolves. His "nada" prayer illustrates his loss of the conventional religious ideal, but it equally illustrates that the loss has resulted in the broad pessimism which characterizes him.

In "An Alpine Idyll," a peasant mutilates his wife's frozen corpse by hanging a lantern on her lower jaw throughout a winter. The grotesque detail contrasts with the attitudes of the two young characters who are the observers. The peasant's unawareness of having done something unnatural indicates his own absolute coming to terms with death. He tells the priest who questions him, "'Ja, I loved her,' Olz said. 'I loved her fine'" (348). The point is, he has accepted her death. Those who criticize him cannot accept naturally the knowledge of death; in fact for them outward form has all the importance in any situation.

Hemingway also treats the theme of adjustment to contingencies in "Two Tales of Darkness."[14] The first, "A Man of the World," relates the grotesque nature of a man's adjustment to blindness. The character, whose eyes have been gouged in a fight earlier in his life, has created a kind of adjustment out of pride, not self-pity. In spite of the deterioration of his physical and moral state, he has established a buffer between the reality of his situation and true realization through his pride in the knowledge that he has so disfigured his opponent in the fight that the latter cannot appear in public. The adjustment rests upon grotesque irony, and it is not an admirable one.

The second of the Tales, "Get a Seeing-Eyed Dog," depicts the loss of sight and the accompanying loss of old modes and habits of living for the central character. In this story the man is a writer, and he is sensitive to the effect his blindness must have upon his wife. He tries to send her away in order to relieve what he imagines to be her slavish responsibility to him. Her refusal does not constitute a sentimental ending, for he still has not adjusted to the blindness. The final view of his feelings illustrates the small hope for an eventual coming to terms with the situation: "But walking down the stairs feeling each stair carefully and holding to the banister he thought, I must get her away and get her away as soon as I can without hurting her. Because I am not doing too well at this. That I can promise you. But what else can you do? Nothing, he thought. There's nothing you can do. But maybe, as you go along, you will get good at it."[15]

In "Fathers and Sons," Hemingway describes an older Nick Adams who re-examines his life. The presence of Nick's son in the story points out the theme of reconcilement of the past with the present and the future. It is an appropriate conclusion to Hemingway's arrangement of *The First Forty-Nine*. The most relevant point of the story to the theme of individuation is that it asks some important questions concerning the possibility of continuity for man. Nick reassesses the learning experiences he has undergone as a youth and the role which his father played in that learning. The father taught him things about hunting, but he failed to give him the more vital information that leads a child into adulthood. The real learning came from the experiences with the environment. Nick evidences his concern for the loss suffered, and he indicates the need for reconcilement in a remark to his son, who has just told him, "'Well, I don't feel good never to have even visited the tomb of my grandfather.' 'We'll have to go,' Nick said. 'I can see we'll have to go'" (499).

The final acceptance of the father figure as necessary to the continuity of life is in reality a reconcilement with the forces of authority. No matter what the reason for the original loss of attachment, Nick finally becomes at one with the father and thereby becomes the father himself. The reconcilement represents a return from isolation and dissociation. Nick's acceptance of his own father is tantamount to his becoming a self-realized man. He is a man who recognizes that he too will pass away and that the only hope for personal immortality rests in the continuity from his father to his own son.

The stories with a strong hero as the central character illustrate the falseness of the notion that Hemingway projects in his fiction a view of life typified by the "nada" prayer of "A Clean Well-Lighted Place." To assign nihilistic tendencies to the author because of the attitudes of the characters in the stories is to misread Hemingway. Too often his objectivity and naturalistic style is confused with authorial viewpoint. Analysis of the "hero" stories amply reveals a well-formulated and systematic ideal based on the notion that man ought to be true to himself. Throughout the short stories Hemingway depicts man in his strife with contingent forces in the local environment and in the cosmos. The true man of ideals may be in harmony with ultimate causality, but in Hemingway's stories his doom in this world is a foregone conclusion. The man who can get along in the world, however, is also represented. He is the one who recognizes the hopelessness of following the ideal to its logical extension. These adjusted ones are the characters like Zurito and Wilson, but they are not the true Hemingway heroes. Only those who grasp the ideal and follow it, whether through innocent ignorance or through full acknowledgement of the ideal, are truly the "undefeated" in Hemingway's terms.

MAKE IMPORTANT
lOSE UNION!

Notes

With the exception of "Two Tales of Darkness," all references to Hemingway's short stories will be from *The Short Stories of Ernest Hemingway* (New York: Charles Scribner's Sons, 1954). Page numbers from this edition will be cited within the text.

Chapter I

1. Ernest Hemingway, *Green Hills of Africa* (New York: Charles Scribner's Sons, 1953), 21.

2. *Ibid.*, 109.

3. Ernest Hemingway, *Death in the Afternoon* (New York: Charles Scribner's Sons, 1954), 2.

4. Ernest Hemingway, "Introduction," *Men at War* (New York: Berkley Publishing Corp., 1958), 7.

5. Hemingway, *Death in the Afternoon*, 2.

6. Hemingway, *Green Hills of Africa*, 26-27.

Chapter II

1. Philip Young, *Ernest Hemingway*, University of Minnesota Pamphlets on American Writers, No. 1 (Minneapolis: University of Minnesota Press, 1959), 4 ff. Carlos Baker, *Hemingway: The Writer as Artist* (Prince-

ton: Princeton University Press, 1956), 127 ff. See also Philip Young, *Ernest Hemingway* (New York: Rinehart and Co., 1952).

2. Joseph Campbell, *The Hero with a Thousand Faces,* Bollingen, XVII (New York: Pantheon Books, 1953).

3. Jesse Weston, *From Ritual to Romance* (New York: Peter Smith, 1941), 21.

4. Carl G. Jung, *Modern Man in Search of a Soul,* trans. W. S. Dell and Cary F. Baynes (New York: Harcourt, Brace and Co., 1948), 189.

Chapter III

1. Young, *Ernest Hemingway* (New York, 1952), 28 ff.

Chapter IV

1. T. S. Eliot, *The Waste Land,* in *The Complete Poems and Plays* (New York: Harcourt, Brace and Co., 1952), ll. 340-45.

2. Campbell, *The Hero with a Thousand Faces,* 17.

3. *Ibid.,* 53.

4. Young, *Ernest Hemingway* (New York, 1952), 13.

5. William Bysshe Stein, "Love and Lust in Hemingway's Short Stories," *Texas Studies in Literature and Language,* III (1961), 239.

6. James Clark Maloney, "The Origin of the Rejected and Crippled Hero Myths," *The American Imago,* XVI (1959), 276.

7. Stein, "Love and Lust in Hemingway's Short Stories," 234.

8. For a discussion of this aspect of the Christ story, see M. Esther Harding, *Journey into Self* (New York: Longmans, Green and Co., 1956), 133.

Chapter V

1. Baker, *Hemingway: The Writer as Artist*, 153.

2. Young, *Ernest Hemingway* (New York, 1952), 137-38.

3. John Killinger, *Hemingway and the Dead Gods: A Study in Existentialism* (University of Kentucky: University of Kentucky Press, 1960), 18.

4. For a full account of the significance of the ritualistic activities, see Stein, "Ritual in Hemingway's 'Big Two-Hearted River,'" *Texas Studies in Literature and Language*, I (1960), 555-61.

Chapter VI

1. Alexander Pope, "An Essay on Man," *Alexander Pope: Selected Poetry and Prose*, ed. William K. Wimsatt, Jr. (New York: Rinehart and Co., 1956), II, ll. 217-20.

2. *Ibid.*, II, ll. 1-2.

Chapter VII

1. Carl G. Jung, *Psychology and Alchemy*, trans. R. F. C. Hull, Bollingen, XII (New York: Pantheon Books, 1953), 7.

2. Carl G. Jung, *The Development of Personality*, trans. R. F. C. Hull, Bollingen, XVII (New York: Pantheon Books, 1954), 180.

3. *Ibid.*

4. *Ibid.*, 181.

5. Hemingway, *Death in the Afternoon*, 16.

6. *Ibid.*, 96.

7. *Ibid.*, 97.

8. *Ibid.*, 98.

9. *Ibid.*, 4.

10. *Ibid.*, 9.

11. *Ibid.*, 34.

12. *Ibid.*, 86.

13. Baker, *Hemingway: The Writer as Artist*, 191-92.

14. Hemingway, *Two Tales of Darkness, The Atlantic*, CC (Nov. 1957), 64-68.

15. *Ibid.*, 68.

INDEX

THE HERO IN HEMINGWAY'S SHORT STORIES

This first book-length study of Ernest Hemingway's short stories uses modern psychological procedures to show that the stories are structured upon the theme of individuation — the quest for self-illumination.

In his short stories, written over a period of years, Hemingway has catalogued the disillusionments of contemporary man in his struggle to come to terms with a world he cannot understand. His central characters constantly face contingent forces in life, and their attempts to reconcile the irrationality of these intrusions form the underlying motivation for action. Joseph DeFalco's viewpoint of those characters provides a new statement about the Hemingway hero: only a successful few, those who master and control the contingencies of life, emerge triumphant in crucifixion. Those who cannot overcome these dislocations resort to compromise, and those who can neither compromise nor conquer are the alienated and isolated ones.

Dr. DeFalco's emphasis is on the relationship between structure and theme, and psychological symbolism provides the means of exploring this relationship. Hemingway's openly avowed intent to translate factual data into fiction, and thereby re-create the essence of true-life experience, combines with his belief in certain elemental patterns of human action and thought to become the means by which his art achieves its expression. The symbolic function of details as revealed through the use of characters, episodes, patterns of imagery, and isolated symbols integrates with Hemingway's surface narrative technique of furthering the plot development. The resulting thematic design projects the implications of a character's struggle with life into the realm of the psychological conflicts of all men.

Dr. DeFalco is Associate Professor of English at Marquette University, and he has taught at Washington and Jefferson College and the University of Rhode Island. His articles have appeared in *Literature and Psychology*, *Walt Whitman Review*, *Southern Folklore Quarterly*, and *Topic*.

UNIVERSITY OF PITTSBURGH PRESS